National Transportation Policy:
A Study of Studies

National Transportation Policy: A Study of Studies

Harvey A. Levine
R.L. Banks & Associates, Inc.

Lexington Books
D.C. Heath and Company
Lexington, Massachusetts
Toronto

Library of Congress Cataloging in Publication Data

Levine, Harvey A.
  National transportation policy.

  1. Transportation and state—United States. 2. Transportation—
Research—United States. I. Title.
HE206.2.L48   353.008′7   78-7156
ISBN 0-669-02393-0

Published simultaneously in Canada

Printed in the United States of America

International Standard Book Number: 0-669-02393-0

Library of Congress Catalog Card Number: 78-7156

Contents

List of Figures

List of Tables

Preface

Section 154 of the Federal-Aid Highway Act of 1976 established the National Transportation Policy Study Commission, to "make a full and complete investigation and study of the transportation needs and of the resources, requirements, and policies of the United States to meet such expected needs." Tacking the creation of a broad study group onto a highway appropriations bill speaks for itself, and as a critical student of transportation policy, I originally viewed the prospective research with a jaundiced eye. My early doubts were reinforced by the charge of Congress to "evaluate the relative merits of all modes of transportation in meeting our transportation needs." It seemed to me that once again transportation needs and modal assistance were to be synonymous; that once again another federal study was going to rationalize increased public involvement in the private sector; and that once again a policy group would support a coordinated and balanced transportation system, waterway users charges, and further research—among others, all popular and safe recommendations emanating from many past policy studies.

My skepticism was soon replaced with approval, appreciation, and admiration, when the Study Commission engaged my firm, R.L. Banks & Associates, Inc., and myself as Project Director, to conduct an investigation of historic research on national transportation policy. I not only respected the commission's choice of a consultant, but approved of linking current policy with past research on the subject. For some time I had suspected that much could be learned from studying past policy research, and after identifying over 500 transportation policy studies since 1886 (including congressional hearings) and comprehensively evaluating thirty-six major efforts, my suspicions were confirmed. Yet, conclusions regarding issue identification, research approach, and recommendations left a major question unanswered. How has historic policy research affected national transportation policy? Because my firm's contract with the commission had terminated, I pursued this subject independently and combined the ensuing analysis with my prior research for the Study Commission. Hence, this book includes an historical analysis of research on national transportation policy, an evaluation of such research, the linkage of policy research to policy formulation, and suggestions for making future research less wasteful and more relevant.

While I am totally responsible for the research, findings, and conclusions of this book, including accuracy of all technical aspects, I have benefited from the assistance of several individuals. Dr. Nai Chi Wang, also of R.L. Banks & Associates, Inc., helped with the research included in Chapter 2. Furthermore, I was aided in locating research documents by Kenneth R. DeJarnette, Congressional

Research Service, Library of Congress, and Frank Licord, Interstate Commerce Commission.

Finally, my special and continued appreciation to my wife, Ferne, and children, Howard and Melissa, who provided the atmosphere conducive to researching and writing in a home environment.

1 Introduction

The term "national transportation policy" is at best a vague concept. Each of the three words comprising the phrase connotes a host of implicit and controversial assumptions; when joined, their meaning takes on an elusiveness of geometric proportions. Countless research efforts have been devoted to the identification, explanation, organization, development, evaluation, and promotion of public policy toward transportation—often identified as national transportation policy.

Dissecting the phrase, the word "national" implies that transportation need have countrywide comparability. A national transportation system may be apparent to the traveler driving on a national interstate system of highways, at a federally determined maximum speed of 55 miles per hour, in an automobile whose tires, emission system, windows, and seat belts have all been designed to meet national standards. What may not be so apparent to this individual is that the federal government owns a railroad in Alaska, regulates the service and rates of the various transport modes, operates the air-control systems at airports, and maintains the nation's inland waterways. Even more obscure to the individual is that federal income taxes are used to operate railroad passenger trains between Los Angeles and New Orleans; to subsidize commuter transit systems in Washington, D.C., and San Francisco; to construct and operate a people-mover in Morgantown, West Virginia; and to fund esoteric university research throughout the country. The increasing scope and level of federal involvement in transportation is well documented,[1] and the subject continues to be hotly debated. Still, the word "national" indicates that the federal government has a significant role to play in planning, organizing, and controlling the nation's transportation resources.

"Transportation" at first glance appears to be a rather universally accepted word, defined by Webster as "means of conveyance or travel from one place to another."[2] However, it is unlikely that many people consider walking, bicycling, or even motorcycling as components of transportation. There is probably even an obscurity about such capital-intensive businesses as barge operations and pipelines being a part of the transportation infrastructure. In fact, there are those who consider freight movement as being transportation, with passenger travel falling under the category of "traffic." This latter interpretation is contrary to titles and responsibilities of many industrial shipping executives—for example, traffic managers. The point is that transportation is such a broad term that all movement can logically be aggregated under its heading—even electricity

1

and other forms of power—and accepting the broad definition of transportation implies an acceptance of the myriad of users, including such special-interest groups as large industrial shippers, rural consumers, elderly, handicapped, low-income residents, racial minorities, small retailers, intercity travelers, and urban commuters, among others. This incomplete list can be further segmented into subcomponents (markets) such as intercity travelers afraid to fly, large industrial shippers located on a railroad line, commuters not owning automobiles, etc. These groups often have different, and at times conflicting, needs. Even where needs are in harmony, financial resources are limited and allocation choices must be made. In essence, within the context of national transportation policy, just what modes of transport and which groups of users should be considered are comprehensive and difficult issues to resolve.

Finally, the word "Policy" assumes that a plan can be devised to affect transportation so that regulatory and promotional decision-making will be consistent and based on the achievement of stated objectives. According to leading management experts, "policies tend to predecide issues, avoid repeated analysis and consideration of general courses of action, and give a unified structure to plans. . . ."[3] Thus, the exercise of policy assumes that goals can be readily identified, evaluation criteria can be explicitly stated, and a harmonious organization can be formed to work toward the common good. In transportation, the common good is synonymous with public interest, and this term represents the difficult-to-determine net of conflicting interests among regions, interest groups, and economic-social-political standards.

In conclusion, conceptually the term national transportation policy is so fraught with definitional problems that effective practical application is highly problematical. Identifying transportation issues of national significance, interrelating such issues within a comprehensive system, and developing methods for resolving major issues have been part and parcel of thousands of articles, books, research studies, and congressional hearings. Still, national transportation policy remains as much an enigma as ever. Past, as well as contemporary, studies have reached the ineluctable conclusion that transportation policy is uncoordinated, imbalanced, inconsistent, and/or incoherent; recommendations are often in the form of suggestions, and a call for additonal research is ubiquitous. Even a recent congressional study[4] advocated additional research in such often-researched areas as railroad electrification, railroad financing, railroad rate regulation, truck size and weight limitations, pipeline-railroad competition, railroad passenger service, and federally aided highways.

It is the contention of this author that answers to many questions on the major transportation issues of national interest may be found in the anatomy within, and relationships among, previous analyses of such issues. Hopefully, this study, which tests the hypothesis stated above, will not only aid in the way national transportation policy issues are studied in future years, but will also provide public decision-makers with the opposite questions for focusing on the root causes of policy ineffectiveness.

National Transportation Policy

The federal government has been active in transportation planning and development since 1789, when the first Congress initiated a subsidy mechanism to promote the development of an American merchant fleet by providing for a 10 percent reduction in customs duties on imports reaching American shores in U.S. vessels and by imposing a tonnage tax in favor of American shipping. Still, it was not until 151 years later that a national transportation policy was explicitly stated, as a preamble to the Transportation Act of 1940 (amendment to the Interstate Commerce Act of 1887). This policy statement, unchanged to this date, reads as follows:

It is hereby declared to be this national transportation policy of the Congress to provide for fair and impartial regulation of all modes of transportation subject to the provisions of this Act, so administered as to recognize and preserve the inherent advantages of each; to promote safe, adequate, economical, and efficient service and foster sound economic conditions in transportation and among the several carriers; to encourage the establishment and maintenance of reasonable charges for transportation service, without unjust discrimination. Undue preferences or advantages, or unfair or destructive competitive practices; to cooperate with the several States and the duly authorized officials thereof; and to encourage fair wages and equitable working conditions;—all to the end of developing, coordinating, and preserving a national transportation system by water, highway, and rail, as well as other means, adequate Postal Service, and of the national defense. All of the privisions of this Act shall be administered and enforced with a view to carrying out the above declaration of policy.[5]

Since 1940 the national transportation policy statement has been criticized countless times by a plethora of individuals and organizations at all levels of private and public enterprise. Entire books have been written on the subject, with the overwhelming consensus concluding that the policy statement leaves major national planning questions unanswered. Even at the highest level of public transportation planning, the National Transportation Policy has been criticized; former DOT Secretary Claude Brinegar labeled it "vague and elusive,"[6] and current Secretary Brock Adams, while a Congressman from the State of Washington, referred to it as "the Abominable Snowman."[7]

The stated, alleged transportation policy has been critically evaluated from varied perspectives, with the most evident emanating from the ICC—the regulatory agency largely responsible for adhering to such policies in its decisions. Paraphrasing an ICC Commissioner,[8] major difficulties in interpreting and enforcing the policy statement are as follows:

Lawfulness of Rates: There are so many contradictory considerations that the ICC must take into account in passing on the lawfulness of rates, that the commission is like a tightrope walker—"there is plenty of room for a spill"—contradictions such as giving weight to both economical transportation and adversely affecting traffic of other carriers and/or modes.

Inherent Advantage: In protecting the inherent advantage of all modes, does such an advantage refer to cost, service, or what? If cost and service, what weights should be given to each? If cost, which costs: full costs or out-of-pocket (direct) costs?

Destructive Competition: How can the commission prevent destructive competition, encourage competiton, and preserve inherent advantages—all at the same time? How can economical transportation be preserved and in fact promoted, while preventing unfair or destructive competition?

Adequate and Efficient Transportation: To achieve these goals, should traffic be allocated among the most efficient carriers? How should efficiency be defined relative to government promotion of certain modes and facilities?

The above inconsistencies in the policy statement, and others, are identified in the so-called Doyle Report,[9] as are inconsistencies in the execution of the law, and in the substantive law of transportation. In view of these inconsistencies, the Doyle Report concludes that transportation policy reflects "a general program of preserving the status quó which is in direct opposition to the overall objective of a dynamic transportation system which can best serve the economy and defense of the country."[10] The report then recommends that a revised National Transportation Policy statement be adopted, giving more emphasis to privately owned carriage within a common-carrier framework.

What the Doyle Report and other critics of the policy statement fail to realize (or at least explicitly state) is that the written statement of policy is somewhat irrelevant to the public-policy, decision-making process within the transportation arena. This irrelevancy is founded on a two-fold premise. First, the policy statement is not actually an expression of policy, but is rather an incomplete listing of goals. Carrier efficiency, adequate service, and safe transportation are national objectives; they are not guidelines for decision-making. Second, as long as the supposed policy statement is broad and harmless enough not to present significant barriers to regulatory and promotional planning, public policy toward transportation will continue to be based on political considerations and individual agency interpretation of objectives, policies (criteria), and strategies. National transportation policy existed prior to the 1940 statement and continues to flourish on an individual ad hoc basis and in an environment where both promotional and regulatory agencies lack intramodal and intermodal coordination.

To summarize, this study examines the roots, structure, and conclusions of past studies addressing at least some major segment of national transportation policy, so that an effective framework can be developed for identifying and resolving significant transportation issues. The policy addressed is not the 1940 statement (of goals) discussed above, but rather the aggregation of federal aid and control of the entire transportation system. No matter how fragmented, inconsistent, contradictory, and/or unidentifiable, national transportation policy is what the federal government does—not what it should do.

The Problem: Relating Research to Decision-making

If effective transportation policy is to be developed and implemented, then a comprehensive framework of issue evaluation will have to be identified, recognized, and accepted. More specifically, it is imperative that transportation research be related to the decision-making process if "good"answers are to be found for the "right" questions. Analogous to the axiom that "when you don't know where you're going a lot of roads will get you there" are the multitudes of transportation research projects which are redundant, irrelevant, unsupported, and/or ignored. Furthermore, many studies reach conclusions which could have been preconceived—for example, that additional research is desirable, proper data were not available to arrive at anything more than inferences, and that transportation goals have not been adequately identified. Other studies conclude the obvious—that on economic grounds AMTRAK is undesirable, that commuters prefer private automobiles to mass transit, and that direct railroad costs are difficult to measure because of the common and joint nature of such costs.

Probably the most perplexing and frustrating problem of transportation research occurs when what appears to be sound research does not induce correspondingly sound decisions, or correspondingly, when decisions are made without the knowledge of supportive research. How often one hears that a subject has been "studied to death," as yet another study on the same subject begins. Or how about the extreme opposite case, where public policy results in recommended changes in transportation legislation, based on little more than intuition? Furthermore, there are instances where study inadequacies lead to further study, and further inadequacies, until the subject of study becomes so entwined in the adversary environment that political compromise is the sole resolution. Many of these types of suspicions are an integral part of the transportation research community, but their presence has never been comprehensively documented.

This book traces the historical relationships between transportation research of a national scope, and public policy at the same level. It identifies and evaluates what the author believes are the key studies on broad issues of national transportation policy from 1886 through 1977. It determines the origins of each major study, major issues identified, derivation of issues, recommendations, and relationship of the study to the transportation environment during the time of the research. These studies were analyzed and compared without a preconceived notion or suspicion of prospective results. Rather, it was expected that by categorizing and conducting a cross-sectional analysis of major studies, that certain patterns and relationships would emerge. Specific examples might include such factors as: the types of issues identified by various categories of studies; lead time between issue identification and resolution; repetitiveness of study components, including recommendations; identification of research methods; and rationale for undertaking the research. What would hopefully evolve from the above analyses would be a set of conclusions leading to an identification of the root causes adversely affecting the resolution of national transportation policy issues. Fortunately, this expectation was realized.

Identification of Major Studies

One of the major tasks requisite to study analysis was determining which prior transportation research studies warranted subsequent evaluation. Transportation is one of those eclectic subjects shared by, among others, economists, engineers, planners, lawyers, sociologists, historians, marketeers, psychologists, and statisticians. Thus, thousands of articles, books, research studies, and congressional hearings have addressed transportation issues, filling the literature with an abundance of material. The chore at hand was to determine which studies deserved designation as "major," relative to national transportation policy and policy issues.

Four broad factors were adopted as criteria for determining whether or not a study was of national transportation import. First, the comprehensiveness of research was considered. Large-scale studies by presidential advisory boards and congressional committees were automatically accepted as significant, as were several textbooks and other research studies solely devoted to the subject of national transportation policy. In other cases judgment prevailed, although if a study was marginal it was included in the initial listing of potentially major studies. Consequently, the preliminary listing of major comprehensive studies includes some thirteen reports comprised of nine efforts by the federal government, three books, and one individual's treatise on the national transportation policy statement. The thirteen studies are listed and briefly identified in table 1-1 below; more detailed descriptions and discussions are presented in the following chapter. With the exception of the 1936 book and 1945 treatise as identified below, the remaining comprehensive studies are described in detail in Appendix A.

A second selection criterion was the stature of the research team relative to the scope of subject matter. In essence, where researchers of national prominence and exposure addressed at least some major facets of national transportation policy, ensuing studies were included on the preliminary list. As shown

Table 1-1
Comprehensive Transportation Policy Studies

Year	Brief Identification	Type of Study
1886	Cullom Report	Congressional study preceding Act of 1886
1933	Moulton Report	Presidential study of board policy
1933–40	Coordinator's Reports	Federal Coordinator of Transportation's reports on regulation and promotion
1936	"A National Transportation Policy"	Early book on the subject of national policy
1942	"Transportation and National Policy"	First postpolicy statement report by National Resources Planning Board
1944	BIR Report	Broad study of federal aid by Board of Investigation and Research
1945	"Our National/Transportation Policy"	Author's analysis of 1940 policy statement
1949	"National Transportation Policy"	Often-referenced book by Dearing and Owens
1960	Mueller Report	Broad study by Department of Commerce
1961	Doyle Report	Congressional study of national policy
1966	"National Transportation Policy"	Noted book by Norton
1977	Trends and Choices	Comprehensive report by Department of Transportation
1977	Magnuson Report	Congressional study of domestic transportation

below in table 1-2, ten such studies were identified, with most being government investigations of the formal organization and intergovernmental relations of public regulatory and promotional agencies. Most of the others addressed the question of regulatory effectiveness (specifically, the ICC), and one focused on a national plan for railroad mergers. The First Hoover Report and the Saywer Report are discussed in detail as part of Appendix A.

A third group (and lower level) of studies included on the preliminary-analysis list consisted of contemporary studies of significant public exposure. Eight such studies were identified; with slight exception, they focus on the desirability of continued federal economic regulation of transportation. Thus, they are limited because they fail to address the promotional side of public involvement in transportation development. Presented in table 1-3 below, these studies are more narrow than previously identified research efforts, and supplement other contemporary reports already listed.

Table 1–2
Other Major Transportation Policy Studies

Year	Brief Identification	Type of Study
1921	Ripley Report	ICC plan on railroad consolidation
1931	Sharfman Study	Academician's analysis of ICC
1949	First Hoover Report	Study of government organization by presidential commission
1949	Sawyer Report	Broad policy study by Department of Commerce
1955	Second Hoover Report	Study of government organization by presidential commission
1955	Weeks Report	Broad policy study by presidential committee headed by Secretary, Department of Commerce
1960	Landis Report	Report on government organization by Department of Commerce
1970	Nader Book	Critical evaluation of ICC by leading consumer advocate
1971	Ash Council Report	Study of government organization by presidential commission
1974	Advisory Commission Report	Study of urban transportation by Federal Advisory Commission

Fourth, and finally, several studies that fit under the classification of odds-and-ends were included in the initial list—each for a specific reason. For instance, a 1938 report by the Transportation Association of America was included to determine the viewpoints of carrier representation during the period just prior to the passage of the 1940 policy statement. The 1946 views of the U.S. Chamber of Commerce were examined to obtain an additional postwar perspective from the business community. A 1972 policy paper by the American Association of State Highway and Transportation Officials is the initial comprehensive policy statement of that organization. An academician's economic analysis of the Interstate Commerce Act in 1975 relates to the other studies of regulation during the past decade. And a 1977 study by the Canadian government on transportation issues in that country would lend itself to comparative analysis. All of the studies in this fourth category have little significance by themselves, but, woven into the cross-sectional evaluation of other studies, may add meaning and perspective. These five reports are listed below in table 1–4.

The selection of thirty-six studies for detailed evaluation does not mean that each study was given equal weight, and thus received a similar degree of analysis. Rather, the comprehensive policy studies were given proportionately more attention than more narrow research efforts, and reports such as those in the odds-and-ends category were only briefly evaluated. Furthermore, there are virtually

Table 1–3
Contemporary Studies Receiving Public Exposure

Year	Brief Identification	Type of Study
1969	Friedlaender Book	Well-known book discussing cost of economic regulation
1972	Moore Study	Book quantifying cost of regulation
1975	CAB Study	Regulatory agency's analysis of economic control
1975	CAB Staff Report	Regulatory agency's discussion of regulatory reform
1975	ICC Blue-Ribbon Report	Regulatory agency's self-evaluation
1975	Mitre Report	Consultant's overview of transportation
1976	ICC Cost-Benefit Study	Regulatory agency's attempt to quantify costs and benefits of regulation
1977	Justice Report	Executive-branch study of regulated ocean shipping industry

thousands of other sources of transportation research where simple identification was acceptable for bolstering inferences and conclusions reached in this study. For example, hundreds of congressional hearings on matters of national transportation policy have been identified for the 1886–1977 time period. These hearings range from narrow subjects such as "Regulation of Railroad Rates" (1904) to the broader issue of "Civil Aviation" (1934), the multi-modal issue of "Common Ownership" (1957), and the system-wide subject of "Regulatory Reform" (1976). What is noteworthy about these hearings is their relationships to major research studies—in particular, their timing, acceleration, subject

Table 1–4
Miscellaneous Transportation Studies

Year	Brief Identification	Type of Study
1938	TAA Viewpoints	Views of national transportation policy by Transportation Association of America
1946	Chamber of Commerce Viewpoints	Views of transportation concerns
1972	Analysis of IC Act	Academician's economic analysis of Interstate Commerce Act
1975	AASTO Viewpoints	National transportation policy by American Assn. of State Highway and Transportation Officials
1977	CTC Report	Discussion of Canadian transportation issues by Canadian Transport Commission

content, repetitiveness, and comprehensiveness. Transportation is the concern of a number of Senate and House committees as noted below:

> *Senate Committees*: Appropriations; Banking, Housing, and Urban Affairs; Commerce, Science, and Transportation; Environment and Public Works; Governmental Affairs; and Judiciary.

> *House Committees*: Appropriations; Banking, Finance, and Urban Affairs; Government Operations; Interstate and Foreign Commerce; Judiciary; Merchant Marine and Fisheries; Public Works and Transportation; and Ways and Means.

Aside from congressional hearings, three other types of transportation research studies were employed in the analysis. First, relevant articles published within the past fifteen years were located in fifteen to twenty journals addressing national transportation issues, and detailed identification, trend, and comparative analyses were conducted for articles in the following publications: *Transportation Journal, ICC Practitioners' Journal, Transportation Research Forum Proceedings*, and *Traffic Quarterly*. Second, studies by universities, single researchers, government agencies, and private-sector interest groups were identified from an extensive literature search. Contracts were made with carrier and shipper associations, as well as the following state and local government groups: Council of State Governments, National League of Cities—transportation; National Association of Counties; National Governors Conference; American Association of State Highway & Transportation Officials; Highway Users Federation; American Road & Transportation Builders; and New England Regional Commission. Third, fifty-one responses by various transportation interest groups were analyzed; these rankings and discussions of national transportation policy issues were in response to requests by the National Transportation Policy Study Commission in early 1977—a commission established in 1977 by the 94th Congress to study transportation "needs, resources, requirements and policies of the United States" through the year 2000.

In total, about 600 transportation studies (including congressional hearings and books) and over 1,100 articles were referenced. Together with the responses to the inquiry of the National Study Commission, and other peripherally related material, about 2,000 historic documents concerned with some aspect of national transportation policy were identified.

Study Organization

Chapter 2 identifies major research studies of at least some aspect of national transportation policy dating from 1886. The congressional report in 1886 was chosen as the base study because it resulted in the initial federal legislation to regulate interstate commerce. Hundreds of studies (including congressional hearings) are identified; thirty-six are briefly discussed and twelve comprehensive efforts are examined in detail, comprising Appendixes A-1 through A-12. Prior studies are introduced within five chronological time frames, and congressional hearings are identified within these same periods in Appendixes B-1 through B-5. Featured highlights of historic studies include background data (that is, what initiated the study), issue derivation, identification of issues, conclusions, and recommendations.

Chapter 3 develops a framework for identifying, classifying, and relating transportation issues addressed in prior research studies—a framework similarly applicable to issue analysis in the future. Initially, ubiquitous problems inherent in transportation research are presented to serve as the parameters for ensuing classification. Issues are then grouped into decisions, impact, and goal categories. Identified goals center on economic efficiency, national defense, energy conservation, environmental impact, safety, and equity. Chapter 3 utilizes traditional issues identified from the literature search to demonstrate the placement of such concerns within the suggested framework. In essence, this chapter presents an analytical process for determining what the "right" questions are for problem-solving and decision-making, and concludes that too much effort has traditionally been expended on seeking "good" answers to "wrong" questions.

An overview of national transportation policies is presented in Chapter 4 in order to relate research to the trends, scope, and magnitude of federal involvement in transportation. After the term "subsidies" is defined in its broadest context, federal aid to railroads, inland waterways, highways, aviation, and urban transit is examined. Subsequently, federal aid is viewed in the aggregate so that breadth of public control can be appreciated. The chapter concludes with a brief discussion on regulatory trends in order to compare public attitudes toward regulation with promotional philosophy.

Chapter 5 relates essential characteristics of major transportation research studies to promotional and regulatory policies discussed in Chapter 4. Patterns of research approaches are noted, and issue derivation, issue identification, and recommendations are traced across study lines in order to draw conclusions about such matters as repetition, change, and resolution. Two case studies are presented to demonstrate the difficulties of developing national standards for complicated economic matters normally determined in the open market, and for geographic regions having varying demographic and socioeconomic characteristics—essentially different needs, wants, and attitudes. Finally, it is shown that national transportation policies have taken somewhat of a diversionary course whereby promotional activities have been accelerating in the face of a relatively static regulatory environment. A thesis is advanced that this diversion reflects a consistent public policy, and that the research community has exercised a self-serving posture in fostering its continuance.

Finally, Chapter 6 offers some concluding remarks, and a few recommendations, in the hope of developing a more effective research framework to conduct analyses of national transportation policies. A list of tenets and a test of practicality are proposed as prerequisites for comprehensive transportation study. The author believes that acceptance of both elements will help eliminate much of the unneeded (duplicate, irrelevant, biased, etc.) research and will result in study of the root issues implicit in our national transportation policies. Appendixes contain detailed identification and discussion of prior policy studies and by themselves should prove to be a valuable source for transportation researchers.

Notes

1. For instance, see *Federal Aid to Domestic Transportation*, Congressional Research Service, Library of Congress, 77-112 E, May 16, 1977.

2. *Webster's New Collegiate Dictionary*, G. & C. Merriam Company, 1977.

3. Harold Koontz and Cyril O'Donnell, *Principles of Management* (New York: McGraw-Hill Book Company), 1964, p. 75.

4. *Intercity Domestic Transportation System for Passenger and Freight*, Senate Committee on Commerce, Science, and Transportation, 95th Congress, 1st Session, May 1, 1977.

5. *Transportation Act of 1940*, 49 U.S.C., precoding #1, 301, 901, and 1001, September 18, 1940.

6. Testimony before House Transportation Appropriations Subcommittee on National Transportation Policy, March 5-6, 1974.

7. *Ibid.*

8. Rupert L. Murphy, *ICC Practitioners' Journal*, September 1959, pp. 1143-45.

9. *National Transportation Policy*, report of the Committee on Commerce, United States Senate by its Special Study Group on Transportation Policies in the United States, June 26, 1961, pp. 119-53.

10. *Ibid.*, p. 2.

2 Chronology of Research Studies

Transportation historians have traditionally identified and entitled time periods relative to major events. From such landmark changes, eras have emerged—for example, the age of sailing vessels, the age of steam, the age of railroad expansion, the age of the jet, the space age, etc. Each period represents a relatively distinct time frame, and when presented in chronological order symbolizes aspiring technological development in transportation. Students of marketing may equate these technological eras with life-cycle or product-cycle changes, typically identified as innovation, introduction, growth, maturity, saturation, and decline. In reality, technological periods, as with business cycles, tend to overlap and are often difficult to define.

Students of transportation policy also use metamorphic events to determine parameters of time periods, such as legislation, regulatory decisions, and/or judicial action. How policy time frames are classified is unimportant to this study, but identification of legislation framing each range of years is noteworthy since these laws often relate to the chronology of research studies described in this chapter.

It is common to identify the years from 1887 to 1920 as a distinct era because the first federal law to regulate interstate commerce was passed in 1887, and for the next thirty-three years amendments to, and interpretations of, the Interstate Commerce Act (IC Act) were aimed at regulating and controlling potential monopoly (mainly, price discrimination) abuses by the nation's railroads. The Act of 1887 regulated railroad rates and service; the Expedition Act of 1903 provided that, with the designation of the Attorney General, cases under the IC Act would be given precedence in the circuit courts, and that appeals could go directly to the Supreme Court; the Elkins Act of 1903 established that a published railroad rate was the lawful rate, thereby inducing a diminishing of rate-cutting and rebates; the Hepburn Act of 1906 gave the ICC the power to set maximum rates, put teeth into the commission's enforcement authority, strengthened its control over carrier accounts and records, and declared pipelines to be common carriers under the regulatory jurisdiction of the ICC; the Mann-Elkins Act of 1910 provided for specific rate regulation (known as the long-and-short-haul clause) and authorized the commission to hold rate hearings and, if desirable, to suspend rates; the Panama Canal Act of 1912 made it unlawful for a railroad to own a water carrier operating through the Panama Canal; and the Shipping Board Act of 1916 provided for regulation of inland water carriers under the IC Act. Also, during the 1887-1920 period, antitrust legislation in the form of the Sherman Anti-Trust Act (1890), the Clayton Act (1914), and the Federal Trade Commission Act (1914) were passed. Thus, the 1887-1920 era is often characterized in transportation circles as a period of negative regulation.

Beginning in 1920, transportation regulation took a turn to a more positive philosophy with the passage of the Transportation Act of 1920. Largely based on government experience operating the railroad industry during World War I, the act established a rule of rate-making providing for a reasonable return on investment to railroads; also restrictions on carrier combinations and service were liberalized, and interchange provisions were instituted. The spirit of the 1920 act was affirmed by the Emergency Railroad Transportation Act of 1933, whereby the temporary position of Federal Coordinator of Transportation was established to study opportunities for carrier economies, and regulation of both rates and combinations was altered to encourage coordination in transportation. The Motor Carrier Act of 1935 brought motor carriers providing interstate service, with several exceptions, under the IC Act. The Civil Aeronautics Act of 1938 regulated airlines, in much the same manner as railroads and motor carriers, under the authority of the Civil Aeronautics Board (CAB). Freight forwarders were regulated by the Freight Forwarder Act of 1942—an amendment to the IC Act. The Transportation Act of 1940 included a preamble statement of national transportation policy. The interstate system of highways was instituted in 1956 with the passage of the Federal Aid Highway Act. In 1958 the Transportation Act liberalized rate-making restrictions and provided for government guarantees of rail credit. In that same year, the Federal Aviation Act created the Federal Aviation Agency to promote air transportation—an agency which became part of the DOT when this latter cabinet office was created in 1967. Also incorporated into DOT was the Urban Mass Transportation Administration, created by the Urban Mass Transportation Act of 1964. Finally, two other more recent contemporary legislative actions were the so-called 3R (Regional Rail Reorganization) Act of 1973 and the 4R (Railroad Revitalization and Regulatory Reform) Act of 1976—both aimed at rejuvenating the nation's railroads.

From a regulatory perspective, one textbook categorizes transportation time periods as follows:

1. Restrictive Regulations, 1887-1917
    a. The Beginning, 1887-1917
    b. The Doldrums, 1897-1917
    c. Strengthened Regulation, 1906-1917
2. World War I, 1918-1920
3. The Period of Positive Regulation, 1920-date
    a. Constructive Extension of Control, 1920-1928
    b. Increased Flexibility, 1933-1964
    c. Regulatory Reexamination, 1962-date

Superimposing promotional legislation over regulatory time frames may alter classifications somewhat, but not significantly enough to undermine the recognition of change in public policy toward transportation. After all, what is probably the most crucial characteristic of transportation promotion is also the most obvious—the increasing commitment and involvement of the federal government.

Against this background of chronologically categorizing transportation history and legislation, research studies on national policy are classified in the remainder of this chapter. Analogous to legislation, research parameters are framed by study subject, comprehensiveness of analysis, stature of the research team, and prospective evaluation. Research study categories established in this book are: (1) Railroad Regulation, 1886-1932; (2) Regulatory Expansion, 1933-1944; (3) Promotional Development, 1945-1959; (4) The Systems Approach, 1960-1971; and (5) Toward Federal Planning, 1972 to the present.

Railroad Regulation, 1886-1932

On a national scale, transportation research from 1886-1932 was not only rare, it was almost exclusively devoted to railroads. These characteristics exemplified a time when railroads represented the major mode of freight transportation, limited business data were available to researchers, and research monies tended to be allocated for technological, rather than economic (and social), analyses. There were three relatively significant transportation research efforts during these forty-seven years, all conducted by the federal government and each reflecting the public mood of the times.

The most renowned study was the congressional investigation in 1886, preceding the passage of the IC Act the following year. Popularly referred to as the Cullom Committee Report (see Appendix A-1 for detailed description), this congressional study employed public hearings to address a number of preconceived issues relating to railroad rate discrimination. Testimony from representatives of state regulatory agencies and shippers strongly favored federal regulation of railroads, and, based on testimony, such regulation was recommended. The committee's report has traditionally been linked to the passage of the 1887 act.

Once government judgment is superimposed on the decision-making process of the open marketplace, it becomes the subject of continued critical evaluation and controversy. This was certainly the case following the 1887 act, but because research institutions were relatively few in number, regulatory analysis was left pretty much to the government. Several individually sponsored papers were written, such as the one by Joseph Nimmo, Jr., in 1891 entitled "A Proposed Line of Policy for the Correction of Evils Which Now Affect the Railroads of U.S.," and Brooks Adams's 1906 paper, "The President's Railroad Policy (it is based upon a definite anti-monopoly principle)." However, hearings before congressional committees were the main research sources. As shown in Appendix B-1, the several major Senate and House committees devoted to transportation conducted scores of hearings between 1887 and 1920. Many of the hearings focused on the scope of public control of railroads, while others addressed themselves to railroad passenger fares, freight rates, commodity classification, service discrimination, accounting, financing, and consolidation. In fact, relative to railroad mergers, in 1921 Professor W.Z. Ripley prepared a report which formed the basis of ICC plans for nationwide railroad mergers.[2] The commission had found it difficult to enforce the IC Act, especially rate provisions, when both strong and weak railroads were aggregated. Under Section 5 of the act, empowering the ICC to rule on mergers, it prepared a preliminary merger plan addressing the weak-strong problem. Ripley's 1921 plan called for nineteen railroad systems throughout the country, but this figure was modified to twenty-one systems in 1929. The so-called *Ripley Plan* is still referenced in contemporary research of merger alternatives. Other hearings centered on pipelines and water carriers as requisites for legislation affecting both modes as previously mentioned. Finally, in the early 1930s several hearings dealt with motor-carrier regulation, soon to be a reality in 1935.

A second major effort was the *Sharfman Report* in 1931.[3] Undertaken by Professor I.L. Sharfman of the University of Michigan, analysis focused on the effectiveness of the ICC relative to economic efficiency, management principles, and concepts of administrative law. Sharfman's study was the third in a series of research studies funded by the Legal Research Committee, The Commonwealth Fund, New York, begun in 1921 to examine administrative law. The first study was general, and the second focused on the Federal Trade Commission. Sharfman's report interpreted the commission's administrative performance, reviewed its historic performance, and analyzed its opinions and pronouncements. This was the first comprehensive evaluation of the ICC since its establishment in 1887. User and carrier issues (for example, the problems of the railroads) were treated as incidents to the proper understanding and interpretation of the commission's functions and processes. Sharfman concluded that the ICC "achieved a high degree of effectiveness in its own sphere and has contributed substantially to the development of the general essentials of sound regulatory process." He recommended that the ICC be maintained, strengthened, and used as a model for other regulatory agencies.

Finally, in 1933 H.G. Moulton of the Brookings Institution prepared a report reflecting a study of national transportation problems (Appendix A-2). The so-called *Moulton Report* was prepared for the National Transportation Committee, headed by Bernard M. Baruch, and included other individuals of national stature. Data were qualified, rather than quantified, and were abstracted from hearings before the committee, as supplemented by Moulton's staff. The report was substantially influenced by a depression philosophy, and much attention was addressed to reduced regulatory restrictions on railroads. The recommendation for extending regulation to other modes was soon to be realized for motor carriers, airlines, and freight forwarders.

Regulatory Expansion, 1933–1944

The time period from 1933 to 1944 was characterized by expansion of regulation to all modes of interstate transportation. Three major transportation studies, two of which remain landmark research efforts, were conducted amidst such expansion. The first, and probably the most recognized study among transportation analysts, is known as either the *Eastman Studies*, or the *Coordinator's Reports* (Appendix A-3). The office of Coordinator of Transportation was legislated by the Emergency Railroad Act of 1933 and terminated three years later. Joseph B. Eastman, Chairman of the ICC and later referred to as "Mr. Transportation," was appointed Coordinator by President Roosevelt. Under Mr. Eastman's direction, four major reports were issued between 1934 and 1936, as were ten relatively minor reports on the economics of various phases of carrier operations. After termination of the Coordinator's position, four volumes of *Public Aids to Transportation* were released between 1938 and 1940 under Charles S. Morgan's (ICC staff) direction. The aggregation of *Coordinator's Reports* represents the first thorough investigation of intermodal trends and competition after the advent and development of air and motor carrier industries. The studies also assessed relative economic characteristics of various modes, and presented both proponents' and opponents' sides of contemporary controversies. Regulation of railroads was examined in detail, as were public aids to all modes. Furthermore, research and analysis extended to user payments for highways and streets. The scope of research, individual issues identified, analytical procedures, conclusions, and recommendations set the precedent for ensuing government study to this date. Many of the recommendations of the Coordinator's reports have long been implemented, including: extended control over inland water carriers and motor carriers, establishment of joint water-railroad rates, and accelerated study of the entire transportation system.

Concurrent with, and subsequent to, the *Coordinator's Reports*, a number of related papers and articles began to appear in the literature. The 1930s and early 1940s had brought all modes of transportation under regulation, and together with public recognition of the need for a systematic approach to federal aid, researchers took an increasing interest in national policy toward transportation. Following up on his earlier study, Moulton introduced his "Fundamentals of a National Transportation Policy" in 1934,[4] soon followed by Duncan's book of a similar title.[5] While Duncan's book had a distinct railroad orientation, his recommendations, as follows, were broad and, in some cases, not dissimilar to later events: establish national transportation policy stressing coordination and equality; promote adequate facilities preserving all modes; develop equal economic regulation; establish one promotion agency; and develop an efficient and adequate system. Similarly, in 1938, the Transportation Association of America published the results of a three-year study, utilizing data and research of the Joint Commission of Agriculture Inquiry of Congress (1921), and studies of the federal Coordinator. Recommendations were to: create a single regulatory agency, repeal legislation resulting in reduced transportation rates for government, promote railroad consolidation, and exclude transportation from antitrust laws, among several other regulatory adjustments.[6]

Aside from the studies of broad transportation policy, a number of studies on policy aspects relating to specific modes were published during this period of extended regulation. Examples of such studies included several publications on the Motor Carrier Act,[7] Fagg's tracing of the relationship between national transportation policy and aviation,[8] and Locklin's study of motor-carrier regulation.[9] Several other papers addressed the 1930 act and/or congressional intent.[10]

Although far below the comprehensiveness and stature of the *Coordinator's Reports*, a second noted study was the one undertaken by the National Resources Planning Board in 1942 (Appendix A-4). The board was one of several ad hoc groups formed by President Roosevelt for studying and providing data on natural resources during World War II. It identified major transportation issues as needs and recommended upgrading of carrier terminals, the highway system, and airports. Other recommendations were for a single public transportation agency to coordinate planning, public loans and subsidies to railroads, stimulation of railroad consolidation, and federal authority for eminent domain. The report concluded that a balance should be struck between "competitive forces and public controls." One probable reason for the lack of acclaim accruing to this report is due to its abrupt termination. With the ending of the war in sight, the board was terminated in 1944.

The third major study of the 1933–1944 time period was the *BIR Report*, published in 1944 (Appendix A-5). The Board of Investigation and Research was viewed by some as an extension of the Coordinator's Committee. In fact, the *BIR* utilized the *Eastman Studies* and, together with other data and input from public hearings, focused on issues similar to many of those in the Eastman reports. Aside from the popular recommendation to establish a single federal transportation agency, *BIR* suggestions tended to be broad—for example, further study of carrier user payments, government review of railroad mail rates, waterway funding based on economic considerations, and need for more planning.

One specific recommendation worth noting is that of adopting water-carrier user charges. In conclusion, the *BIR Report* is one of those curious studies which seems to have received publicity and stature far beyond its substance and/or contribution to national transportation policy. Possibly because it followed (and referenced) the *Eastman Studies*, or maybe simply because it was the major federal government study of transportation during World War II, the *BIR* study is well known in transportation circles. Yet, the report offers almost nothing new in the way of recommendations, and its analytical techniques for measuring the level of public aid are suspect. In fact, one of the two board members (Webb) concluded that "the staff report ... attempts to interpret the data in such a way as to exaggerate greatly the amount of public aids extended to highway, water, and air transportation, and it makes no effort to balance up the public expenditures with the public benefits derived."

The trend of modal expansion is evident by the subject matter covered in congressional hearings. Two noticeable characteristics result from the list of congressional hearings between 1933 and 1944, as presented in Appendix B-2. First, relatively few hearings on transportation were held during this time, due largely to the war effort and the several government studies that were conducted. And second, subject matter pertained to all modes, and addressed such areas as labor and abandonment of service. Thus, the broad scope of subject matter introduced in congressional hearings during the 1930s was a prelude to future coverage.

Promotional Development, 1945–1959

The end of the war was accompanied by a renewed interest in domestic transportation. Abeyant demand for goods and services was awakened, and, in view of the 1940 National Transportation Policy, establishment of a coordinated national system appeared to be a priority. One study identified the problem of carriers' being subject to regulation by both transportation and antitrust law,[11] while in other instances special-interest groups voiced their interpretations of the policy statement.[12] An entire study was devoted to interpret the phrasing and individual wording of the 1940 policy within the author's definition of public interest and carrier rights; the statement was defended, but numerous guidelines for interpretation were recommended.[13] Then, in 1949, three studies were issued, addressing to varying degrees the organizational role of the federal government in the transportation marketplace.

The *First Hoover Commission Report* (Appendix A-6) was a broad organizational study of the executive branch of government in general and is well known for the professional esteem of committee members, including former President Herbert Hoover as chairman. The study devoted relatively little effort to transportation. It recommended the consolidation of transportation activities under one department, and addressed the organization of regulatory commissions. Two members of the Hoover Commission advocated a single transportation regulatory agency comprised of the ICC, CAB, and FMC. Data were collected mainly from interviews with government personnel and other submissions from individuals experienced in public affiars who were assigned to various commission task forces. A *Second Hoover Commission Report* was issued in 1955,[14] which concentrated on bringing efficiency of business operations to the military. Relevant recommendations were broadly stated: (1) study and revise, where desirable, regulatory policy; (2) ensure proper rules and regulations of government transportation; and (3) unclassified defense data should be submitted to regulatory agencies.

A second study, published as a book in 1949, was basically an addendum to the first Hoover study, and is referenced herein as the *Dearing-Owens Study* (Appendix A-7). Undertaken by two researchers from the Brookings Institution who supplemented the Hoover Commission, the book focused on organizational issues and broad policy concepts. As one of the first scholarly books on national transportation policy after adoption of the 1940 policy statement, *Dearing-Owens* is often referenced as a major policy study outside the realm of federal government investigation. Two organizational recommendations of the study stand out. The inclusion of the Federal Maritime Administration as part of a single promotional agency (DOT) is a suggestion which to this day has not been legislated but remains somewhat popular; the agency is a component of the Department of Commerce. Furthermore, the recommended consolidation of ICC, CAB, and FMC components is a contemporary issue, having gained support from subsequent studies.

The third major research effort in 1949 was the *Sawyer Report* (Appendix A-8), a study prepared by the Department of Commerce at the request of President Truman. As with comprehensive studies, this report focused on co-ordination among federal promotional agencies and between the regulatory and promotional sides of public policy. The final report was brief and of limited impact, although recommendations were explicitly detailed. Major recommendations included the development of: (1) a single federal agency to coordinate transportation promotion, (2) user charges where they did not exist, (3) a modal price structure based on fully distributed costs, (4) railroad consolidation, and (5) fully integrated federal programs of continuing transportation research and cost-benefit analysis. The limited impact of the Commerce study may be attributed to three factors. First, the outbreak of the Korean War in the middle of 1950, only six months after its release, diverted the nation's attention to preparation for the war. Second, the report of the Hoover Commission was released at the same time, and its publicity far exceeded that of the Sawyer study. Third, the report was only intended to be used as a background paper for discussion within the executive branch of the government; the affected industries were not even consulted during the preparation of the report.

Engulfing the three 1949 studies were a host of other research efforts from 1945 through 1959. Textbooks were written on transportation as a functional field,[15] and on the various modes as centers for managerial and public policy concern.[16] National transportation policy remained open to controversy,[17] and continued to be interpreted from the often-contradictory perspectives of adversaries.[18] The transportation industry had matured to a level where its history was being documented,[19] and even the shipper was gaining stature in the research community as a book on traffic management was published for application as a college textbook.[20] Also, two studies by different faculty members of Harvard University[21] aided the acceptance of transportation as a subject worthy of investigation by prominent members of academia. With the transportation industrial complex reaching midlife of operating maturity (especially with the beginning of the Interstate Highway System in 1956), in the 1950s transport research began an elevation toward becoming part-and-parcel of the broader, sophisticated, university-government-industry research community.

Another study warranting mention was a relatively comprehensive effort in 1955 by a presidential advisory group. The group was directed by Secretary of Commerce Weeks, and it was the only large-scale government investigation during the 1950s. Known as the *Weeks Report*,[22] the study focused on two major federal policies requiring (in its view) prompt revision: pricing and the common-carrier system. The study was based on the premises that pervasive transportation competition was desirable, regulation was obsolete, and common carriage was essential. While it did not propose changes in regulation of carrier entry, the *Weeks Report* recommended that a more explicit policy on national transportation be established, that there should be an increased reliance on competitive forces in rate-making, and that impediments to maintenance of a financially strong system of common carriage should be removed. These recommendations may have been too broad to render the study as either effective or of major significance.

Congressional hearings reflected public attention directed toward the airline industry during the postwar era. As shown in Appendix A-3, aviation concern encompassed broad national policy, regulation, operational aspects, loans, and a number of proposed legislative changes; consequently, in 1958 the Federal Aviation Act was passed. Attention to the airline industry was certainly understandable after World War II in view of air capability and the number of pilots available to meet peacetime needs. Similar characteristics were evident in the middle and late 1950s after the war in Korea. Other than the focus on aviation, Appendix B-3 reflects the now-established pattern of congressional interest in a wide variety of transportation subjects, with the usual inclusion of railroad problems, regulatory restrictions, and broad national policy.

The Systems Approach, 1960-1971

During the 1960s transportation researchers devoted increased efforts to determine relationships and trade-offs among entities which had historically been often treated as separate segments. This so-called systems approach to analysis (or management) appears to have spilled over from large industrial shippers where a revolution toward the "total cost concept" was occurring. The systems approach, or total cost concept, dictated that transportation costs be analyzed as part of a total distribution package including transportation, warehousing, inventory control, and order processing. Traffic managers took on new responsibilities and often new titles such as Distribution Manager or Director of Physical

Distribution, and in some cases the distribution function was elevated to a corporate level represented by a vice-president.

On the supply side of transportation research, the systems approach was introduced for analysis among the various modes; between passenger and freight service; among urban development, transit service, and urban goods movements; and ultimately between federal regulation and promotion. The movement started slowly, was highlighted by the creation of the Department of Transportation (DOT) in the late 1960s, and began to reaccelerate in the 1970s with increased availability of data and the intoduction of third-generation (on-line) computers.

The two major studies in the 1960–1971 time frame were both conducted in the earlier years. A report prepared by the Department of Commerce (DOC) at the request of President Eisenhower was issued in 1960, and is referred to herein as the *Mueller Report* (Appendix A-9). This study was undertaken concurrently with the *Doyle Report*, conducted by Congress, but was completed about ten months earlier than the preliminary draft of the Doyle study. Also, in some ways it resembled the *Sawyer Report* (1949); both were prepared by Commerce staff, and the study director of this study also served as one of the consultants who reviewed the *Sawyer Report* (Ernest W. Williams of Columbia University). An appendix, separately issued as the supplement to the report, was designed to disclose the reasoning of the study staff underlying the recommendations adapted in the report by the DOC and to indicate, to some degree, the further course of policy development. The report covered nine broad areas of transportation, including urban problems and needs. Recommendations tended to restate earlier suggestions (similar to those in the *Sawyer Report*), but was stronger in its recommendation for the liberalization of regulatory constraints. The report recommended gradual deregulation of carrier entry restrictions, cost-based rates, and the usual list of user charges, stimulation of railroad consolidations, need for additional planning, etc. The importance of this report, or at least the studies underlying the report, has been recognized by the staff director of the Transportation Study Group who prepared the *Doyle Report*.

The second major study was published in 1961, and was both more comprehensive and noteworthy than the *Mueller Report*. The *Doyle Report* (Appendix A-10) was conducted for Congress by a research staff headed by retired Air Force Major General John P. Doyle. It explored transportation policy from the broad concept of the 1940 National Transportation Policy, and included investigations of urban transit, regional planning, private carriage, supply of freight cars, containerization, and public service to rural areas. Research was undertaken in respect to a set of twelve guidelines, or assumptions, concerning public policy toward transportation, as identified below:

1. Political (promotion): need for well-defined plan considering all modes and accompanying costs.

2. Government ownership: to be avoided, but possible need for public regional ownership of mass transit.
3. Public interest: broad public interest is only legal basis for federal intervention.
4. Economics: deviations from test of economics is necessary, as in defense (general public should bear costs).
5. Competition: level of regulation should by dynamic in response to competitive realities.
6. Equity: all modes must receive equitable treatment from government.
7. Common carriage: should be preserved, but only for those services such carriage can best perform.
8. Timing: need goals and guidance; implementation to be timed to give due notice to parties and minimize undesirable impacts.
9. Dual components of transportation: recognize transportation not only as a service, but also as a power industry—can influence changes in social and economic structure.
10. Bargain transportation: bargain rates not in public interest; cost-related rates needed with provision for reasonable return on investment.
11. National Transportation Policy should not be vague and inconsistent, as is now the case:
    a. Objective of coordination dubious if each mode to realize its "inherent advantages."
    b. Both regulation and promotion should be in policy statement.
    c. The words "preserve" and "preserving" should be left out of policy if flexibility is to be achieved.
    d. Reference to destructive competitive practices often protects a carrier from realizing its inherent advantage.
12. National survival: national system required if government decides to prepare for sneak attack; if not, stop spending funds in unorganized way to meet that contingency.

Aside from the studies by the Coordinator of Transportation in the 1930s, the *Doyle Report* may be the most comprehensive study of national transportation policy. While the Coordinator published many reports and volumes of analyses, the *Doyle Report* is a single volume of comprehensive, detailed, and documented subject matter. Some of the recommendations of the Doyle staff have been implemented—for example, the establishment of DOT, the creation of AMTRAK, liberalization of carrier rate-making, and railroad merger study from a national perspective. In other cases, recommendations made in 1961 are still under consideration today—for example, common ownership, user charges, repeal of right-of-way tax, cost-oriented rates, etc. The report cut across all modes of transportation, considered both freight and passenger issues, and addressed urban transportation as well as regional and national matters. Furthermore, it is one of the few major studies that focused on developing an effective statement of national transportation policy, and, in fact, provided a revised statement to supplant the 1940 policy. With the exception of energy, the *Doyle Report* could be considered a contemporary "bible" for transportation policy-makers and students of national transportation. The *Doyle* and *Coordinator's Reports* (19,308) together represent the two major policy studies throughout transportation history, and, to a major degree, provide a contemporary framework for policy research and development.

Doyle's study overshadowed another report (issued at the same time as the Doyle draft report) undertaken by an executive-branch study team in response to a request by President-elect Kennedy.[23] The new administration believed that many government agencies were ineffective despite sweeping studies which culminated in the *Administrative Procedure Act of 1946*. Major issues identified were: (1) administrative delays, (2) lack of policy formulation, (3) high cost, (4) deterioration in the quality of personnel, and (5) unethical conduct. Data were collected from government agencies, particularly the Bureau of the Budget, and by the staffs of two congressional committees. Of the sixteen specific recommendations, major ones included proposed reorgnaization of the three prime regulatory agencies (ICC, CAB, FMC), and the establishment of a single promotional agency within the executive branch to develop and implement a national transportation policy (DOT).

Within the broadened study context of the 1960s, a curious trend began to form. Possibly spurred by the findings of the *Doyle Report*, inflation, increasing carrier costs, and/or additional data, transportation researchers became more sophisticated and vocal in their criticism of economic regulation. Sampson used the term "obstacles" in describing regulation affecting railroad consolidations,[24] while Miller talked of "institutional frustration"[25] in discussing regulation in general. Articles criticizing transportation regulation appeared in scholarly journals not usually associated with transportation, such as the *American Economic Review*,[26] and entire books were written on the subject.[27] It had become apparent that transportation economics (that is, efficiency) could not be separated from public policy, and research efforts with titles including both words, "economics" and "policy," were not uncommon.[28] In 1969, the questioning of regulation reaccelerated with the publishing of Friedlaender's book, *The Dilemma of Freight Transport Regulation*.[29] Largely based on an earlier paper, and a conference of experts on the subject sponsored by the Brookings Institution, Friedlaender's book made a unique contribution by attempting to quantify the cost of transportation regulation. Estimates of economic loss reflected inefficient traffic allocations, excess capacity, and stifling of technological change. Alternatives to regulatory policies discussed in the book were: cost-based rates, termination of minimum rate regulation, total deregulation, and an end to common-carrier obligation, mergers, and formation of multimodal companies.

Following the trend of regulatory criticism, the much-publicized Nader study of the ICC appeared in book form in 1970, entitled *The Interstate Com-*

merce Commission.[30] Researched by seven law-school students, data relative to the effectiveness and efficiency of the ICC were collected from personal interviews with ICC employees, carriers, shippers, union leaders, and other special-interest groups; formal surveys of attorneys and ICC practitioners; field trips where ICC enforcement procedures were observed firsthand; and reference material including legislation, articles, congressional hearings, and ICC-published information. The report concluded that the ICC should be abolished in its present form and replaced by a new regulatory agency which would remove restrictive barriers to entry, encourage competition, and concentrate on rate discrimination and monopoly pricing. Nader was highly critical of the political nature of the ICC, its protection of inefficient carriers, its policies resulting in monopoly power among certain railroads, and its failure to protect the public from unnecessarily high rates and safety violations among carriers.

The only remaining study of the 1960–1971 period warranting attention was the Ash Council report on executive reorganization in 1971.[31] Appointed by President Nixon, a six-person team under the direction of Roy L. Ash of Litton Industries, Inc., analyzed organizations of seven regulatory agencies in terms of: (1) general organizational concepts for effective administration, (2) transportation regulations, and (3) antitrust enforcement. Evaluations were based on interviews with over 200 experts on regulation, including seminars. The major recommendation was to reduce the number of regulatory agencies from seven to four, including one transportation regulatory agency consisting of the ICC, CAB, and FMC. Also, promotional aspects of the CAB would be transferred to DOT, and the number of FCC commissioners would be reduced from seven to five.

An examination of congressional hearings as presented in Appendix B-4 reveals the broadening scope of federal involvement in transportation between 1960 and 1971. The usual array of hearings on specific issues of modal regulation were evident, as were matters of government organization. However, additional topics were addressed which could fall within the category of transport systems (across modes) planning. It is relatively clear from simply reviewing the subject matter of hearings that it was the intent of Congress to (1) provide loans and/or subsidies to the railroad industry, (2) support the concept of common carriage, (3) maintain the St. Lawrence Seaway, (4) support the development of supersonic transportation, (5) help develop the merchant marine, (6) preserve railroad passenger service, (7) promote vertical type aircraft, (8) establish a federal Department of Transportation with cabinet status, (9) develop an adequate airport system, (10) promote high-speed ground transportation, (11) make regulation more efficient, (12) provide funding for urban transit systems, (13) assist small communities in increasing transportation availability, and (14) develop a federal infrastructure conducive to accelerated transportation planning by modes, political jurisdictions, and other interested parties.

In conclusion, from the perspective of the transportation research community, the country entered the decade of the 1970s with an eclectic posture, and offerings of increased federal resources available for research support.

Virtually no subject was taboo. Exploration into the relationships among service design (vehicle, terminal, etc.), traffic volume, financial stability, costs, regulation, and pricing, among other factors, brought together experts from various fields. The systems approach to transportation research paralleled the age of maturity of the physical system, and the time was ripe for questioning the basis of traditional institutions; regulation was the institution drawing the most attention.

Toward Federal Planning, 1972 to the Present

The early and mid-1970s represented a continuing trend of study undertaken in the previous decade. For instance, much attention remained focused on the issue of transport regulation.[32] Once again a scholar's monolith reviewed ICC law, decisions, and policy, only to conclude that the commission had constrained transportation efficiency.[33] Another more provocative criticism of regulation was raised by Thomas Gale Moore in his study of the cost of federal economic control of surface transportation.[34] Moore identified entry restrictions, monopoly rates, and service inadequacies as components of regulatory cost and espoused the theory that $10–$20 billion might be saved annually be deregulating surface transportation. The deregulation controversy intensified in the 1970s, with a host of papers supporting both sides of the issue.[35]

Much effort was directed toward the rationale of motor-carrier entry restrictions,[36] with Canada (where only Provincial regulation existed) being used as a standard.[37] The ICC was soon stimulated to undertake self-analysis, and after two initial studies[38] it published the infamous *A Cost and Benefit Evaluation of Surface Transport Regulation* in 1976.[39] The study addressed two primary issues: (1) how the data base of Moore's study and certain of his presumptions affect estimates of the cost of ICC regulation, and (2) the significance of the benefits of such regulation. The report concluded that total deregulation of surface transportation would not necessarily solve current problems, nor would it necessarily produce an optimal allocation of resources. Rather, the commission believed that the cost of regulation was overstated by Moore and, in fact, that benefits of regulation could amount to billions of dollars annually. Although this study was not adopted by the ICC, it stirred quite a controversy, and in a May 16, 1977, commentary in *Business Week* (p. 83), the study was characterized as "wrong from the preface."

The above emphasis on motor-carrier (de)regulation should not be construed to mean an absence of research in other regulatory areas, or in among other general transportation subjects. Airline regulation was also studied in detail in the 1970s, and in 1975 the CAB issued a staff report reflecting an inward look at its purpose and effectiveness.[40] This study recommended that protective entry, exit, and public-utility price control in domestic air transportation be eliminated within three to five years by stautory amendment to the Federal Aviation Act, and that safety regulation be maintained and strengthened. Furthermore, the report stated that small community service should be maintained by means of low-bid contracts to qualified bidders. Needless to say, it was rather unique for a regulatory agency to advocate terminating some of its own responsibility. Then, in 1977, the Department of Justice reported on the validity of eccnomic regulation in ocean shipping.[41] Major issues identified were: (1) cartelization, (2) conference system of rate-making, and (3) intraindustry competition. The report mainly engulfed a legal approach in comparing the intent of Congress in passing the Shipping Act of 1916 with the then-present level of competition in the industry. Recommendations were to repeal the 1916 act and to prohibit pooling agreements. The Justice report, as with the CAB study and numerous reports on the ICC, was consistent with a mood toward regulatory reform (liberalization) within the interstate transportation industry.

The broadening research of transportation subject matter was reflected by the array of articles devoted to various interests in four prominent transportation journals from 1972 through 1976. As shown in table 2-1, transportation

Table 2-1
Distribution of Articles by Subject Matter in Four Prominent
Transportation Journals, 1972-1976

Subject Category	Transportation Journal	ICC Practitioner's Journal	TRF Annual Proceedings	Traffic Quarterly
Regulation	20%	42%	8%	1%
Policy/promotion	17	9	3	8
Capital needs, financing	5	9	2	3
Impact analysis	8	11	5	11
Urban	3	–	25	38
Pricing	18	16	5	–
Energy	8	2	3	1
Systems planning, evaluation	5	9	20	18
Technology, computerization	3	–	15	10
International	5	2	6	6
Education and research	8	–	7	4
Labor	–	–	1	–
Total	100%	100%	100%	100%

Note: Percentages are not added across journal lines because of planned bias toward certain subject matter for all, but the *TRF Annual Proceedings*. In essence, neither the journals themselves, nor journal articles, are comparable in terms of significance or random choice of subject.

research in the 1970s encompassed much more than regulatory analysis. In both the *Transportation Journal*, published by the American Society of Traffic and Transportation, and the *ICC Practitioner's Journal*, published by the Association of ICC Practitioners, regulation and pricing were given significant emphasis, but these journals have traditionally focused on such subjects in addressing interests of their membership. This planned direction toward specific subjects is also true for *Traffic Quarterly*, where transit systems are of major concern; thus, it is no surprise to see 38 percent of the articles in the 1972-1976 time period devoted to urban transportation, with only 1 percent focusing on regulation. Undoubtedly, the broadest of the four journals is the *Transportation Research Forum Annual Proceedings*, where all modes and phases of transportation are of interest to members in the forum. As shown in table 2-1, 25 percent of articles from the *Proceedings* were devoted to urban transportation, 20 percent to systems planning and/or evaluation, 15 percent to technology (including computerization), and only 8 percent to regulation. It is also noted that the annual *Proceedings* account for more than three times the number of research papers as do any of the three other journals over a year's period of time. All four publications included articles concerned with broad national transportation policy. The most evident void is in the area of labor, where only 1 percent of articles in the *Proceedings* addressed the subject, and something less than .5 percent existed for the other three publications.

From a transportation research viewpoint, the 1970s are most notable for two major studies published in 1977. These two studies, one by Congress and the other by DOT, are discussed below, but before they are presented three other research efforts of a lesser stature deserve recognition. First, in 1974, the Advisory Commission of Intergovernmental Relations reported on four issues generally relating to urban transportation: (1) dissipated government responsibility for regional transportation, (2) funding criteria, (3) methods of financing, and (4) organizational structure.[42] The study employed a broad approach, reaching general conclusions such as advocating more local planning, improving delivery systems, achieving more balanced federal financing of regional transportation systems, providing for flexible government financing policies, broadening state planning beyond highway needs, and consolidating regulation agencies—this last recommendation being somewhat more specific than the others. Second, in 1975, the Mitre Corporation appraised the national transportation system, addressing urban transit, air travel, and intercity transportation, at a detail appropriate to developing policy.[43] Mitre focused on broad issues that had the "greatest impact on national policy," identified as: regulatory structure, federal aid, economic health of the transportation industry, institutional problems connected with coordinated services, energy, environment, safety, and long-term needs of research and development. Based upon these issues, national policies and priorities were identified along with basic changes needed in the present approach. Three themes were suggested as a framework within which change would be effectively implemented: (1) the need for regulatory reform, (2) the need for organizational and institutional change to provide for more balanced programs and for improved intermodal coordination, and (3) the need for greatly expanded research and development in all phases of transportation. Third, a study was conducted by the Canadian Transport Commission in 1977, which identified trends and issues of the national transportation system in Canada.[44] It is interesting to note the similarity of major transportation issues in Canada and the United States. The Canadian study listed: management-labor relations, rail passenger subsidies, airline financial instability, railroad freight rate structure, uneconomical railroad branch-lines, capital needs, inflation/productivity, and user charges—all not unfamiliar to domestic transport researchers. The commission pointed to changes in the environment such as the rapid escalation of fuel costs, inflation, concern with pollution, a slowdown in the rate of technological change, and declining productivity as major concerns. The study does not make recommendations, but concludes with a statement of future research needs.

Of all the transportation studies from 1970 through 1977, two reports released in 1977 stand out as major research efforts. In the early part of the year, DOT issued what was to become a highly controversial report entitled *National Transportation Trends and Choices* (Appendix A-11). The study was publicized as an extension of the "Statement of National Transportation Policy" which had been submitted to Congress by the Secretary of DOT in 1975. In fact, the report did not recommend explicit policy, or even policy guidelines, but rather was directed toward issue identification. Controversy over the report centered on its limited release by the outgoing Nixon administration, and the new Carter administration's initial refusal to distribute additional copies. The impact of *Trends and Choices* lies in its broad outline of the various transport modes—their operating characteristics, capabilities, and competitive posture. Issues are delineated, and trends and alternatives are enumerated. A common thread throughout the report is that responsibility for transportation planning is so diffused among private and public agencies (federal, state, and local governments) that a single agency cannot work in isolation; planning of the national transportation system requires participation of all government levels and private industry, in addition to widespread public debate. As shown in table 2-2, three scenarios of the transportation environment were presented between 1977 and the year 2000; success, distress, and transformation. Issues were identified relative to each set of assumptions inherent in one of the three scenarios. This rather esoteric, theoretical, and imprecise culmination of the report did little to resolve any major transportation issue, but it appears that this goal was never the intent of the study.

A second and even more significant report issued in 1977 was undertaken by the Senate Committee on Commerce, Science and Transportation. Identified herein as the *Magnuson Committee Report* (Appendix A-12), it resembled a

Table 2-2
Three Scenarios of the Transportation Environment, 1977–2000

Distress

The distress environment is analogous to the present situation whereby external causes adversely affect realization of traditional values. Carriers compete with excess capacity, are alleged to be adversely affected by regulatory constraints, and fear increasing competitive specialization. Similarly, consumers fear urban blight, pollution (air, noise, and water), and inefficient carrier service.

Success

Assuming that traditional values are successfully realized, and that the country continues its industrial expansion while enjoying an efficient transportation system, emphasis will shift almost solely to social problems. Service will be adequate and rates reasonable, so that increased attention will focus on ecology, energy, safety, and other environmental elements.

Transformation

This scenario assumes a shift away from traditional values (such as growth, economic efficiency, and advanced technology) to a desire for small-unit environments—that is, small-neighborhood planning, population dispersion, and generalization. Emphasis will be on interpersonal relationships and quality of life so that, in a sense, a major concern may be too little federal involvement (research, development, etc.), rather than too much control.

miniature *Doyle Report* (1961). The study was directed by a management consulting firm which relied heavily on the literature, and on the knowledge of several transportation consultants supplementing its staff, to identify issues within a modal classification. It appears that the major task, or at least the accomplishment, of the *Magnuson Report* was to develop major issues for further study. Analytical analysis was absent in favor of qualified discussions often presenting both sides of adversary positions on various subject matter. No criteria were presented indicating how issues were determined to be significant, but indications from footnotes were that contemporary research was reviewed in order to determine major problems being faced by each transport mode. The study culmintated with a series of broad conclusions generally falling within one of three categories. First, it was concluded that the federal government lacked a coherent regulatory transportation policy. Second, additional research was recommended in such areas as railroad electrification, recent railroad legislation (3R and 4R Acts), railroad rate regulation, truck size and weight restrictions, inland waterway improvements, coal slurry pipelines, railroad passenger service, and the federal highway program. And, third, it was stated that efficiencies and service improvements could be achieved through increased utilization of equipment and facilities of bus transit operations, and through the development of intermodal transportation by improving urban access to intercity common carriage.

In conclusion, research studies in the 1970s revealed two somewhat contradictory characteristics of contemporary transportation research. On one hand, historic transportation subject matter was addressed in the somewhat traditional manner of offering old arguments on both sides of controversial points, and reaching redundant conclusions steeped in the call for further research. The lack of sound, unified, balanced, cohesive national transportation policy was still being cited;[45] the rationale of economic regulation continued to be hotly debated and studied; and as demonstrated by DOT's *Trends and Choices* and the Magnuson study on surface transportation, both the executive and congressional branches of government were still defining problems and citing the need for additional research. On the other hand, transportation research in the 1970s began to reflect a level approaching total federal immersion in transportation planning. As shown in Appendix B-5, congressional hearings reflected public study of railroad passenger service, freight-service discontinuance (abandonment), employment, accounting, regulations, route structures, and other forms of public aid. Airline and motor-carrier hearings focused on matters similar to those of railroads, although programs of financial assistance were not nearly as extensive. Potential beneficiaries of government subsidies were identified and needs were discussed for such groups as the elderly, handicapped, urban commuters, intercity travelers, and rural residents. And facility planning was not ignored, with attention given to the development of waterways, highways, airports, rail terminals, and ports. The undeniable fact is that transportation policy research and transportation matters discussed by Congress are intertwined. Whether Congress focused on issues evolving from research in the transportation community or whether the opposite occurred is immaterial; probably both cases are true to some extent. What is of import, though, are the lessons emanating from the myriad of transportation studies continually accelerating in both level and scope throughout the country. Much may be learned from trends in research approaches, issue identification, scope of analysis, and, possibly of greatest significance, relating research direction to national transportation policies.

Unanswered Questions

Probably the major observation evident from even the briefest scanning of those transportation policy studies detailed in Appendixes A-1 through A-12 is the recurrence of issues, conclusions, and recommendations. Seemingly, the same old regulatory issues emerge in study after study; to name a few: railroad mergers, cost-based versus value-of-service pricing, abandonment of service, and entry controls. Promotional matters also reemerge since quite naturally, federal criteria for allocating funds, along with carrier financial needs, are the center of discussion. Also, it seems that most comprehensive studies conclude that national transportation policy is elusive at best, a systems approach should be taken in transportation planning, the establishment of DOT makes sense and the Federal Maritime Administration should be incorporated into that agency, user charges should be instituted on inalnd waterways, and more precise criteria are needed in allocating public expenditures. Finally, the all-too-popular call is made for additional research, more comprehensive data, and increased federal planning and financing of the transport system.

In view of recurring, and now predictable, characteristics of major transportation policy studies, a host of questions emerges concerning the value of such reports, and the relationships between policy research and national transportation policy. Why is research needed to make simplistic recommendations for unified federal promotional and regulatory agencies when basic management principles dictate organizational centralization to exploit systems analysis? Why have water-carrier user charges not been implemented after a steady stream of such recommendations throughout the years? What are the benefits of overly broad recommendations such as demands for additional research, "better" data, and more comprehensive planning? Why did it take so long to establish DOT when its formation had been repeatedly supported by research for fifty years prior to its birth in the late 1960s? Why do so many conclusions and recommendations of the *Coordinator's Reports* during the 1930s still appear to be applicable? If certain transportation data are not available, why are affected areas continually studied? Why is it predominantly the federal government which funds and directs extensive policy studies, and can such studies be unbiased? A listing of similar questions can be readily expanded, but the substantive point would remain unchanged. Simply stated, the surface perspective of historic transportation policy research presents time-tested ideas, relatively obvious conclusions, and general recommendations.

Carrying the conclusions regarding the myriad of unanswered questions full circle, other questions come to mind. For instance, are the time-honored issues the important contemporary problems? Were they ever significant? If so, what characteristics have altered their importance? If these issues are of significance, can they be solved? How? At what cost? What is the expected impact from resolution of issues? What geographic regions would be affected? How would service be changed? Where would needed funds be obtained? Etc., etc., etc.

Quite naturally, unanswered questions lead to recommendations for additional research. However, to make such a recommendation herein would be to emulate research that this study has critically evaluated. Rather, the remainder of this book is devoted to seeking the proper framework for meaningful issue identification, analysis, and ensuing solutions. In essence, answers to some of the above questions are sought. The search leads a trail through past policy studies, national regulatory and promotional policies, the adversary nature of public involvement in transportation, and basic principles of economics, management, and logic.

Notes

1. Marvin L. Fair and Ernest W. Williams, *Economics of Transportation and Logistics* (Dallas: Business Publications, Inc.), 1975, pp. 401–402.

2. W.Z. Ripley, "Consolidation of Railroads in the Matter of Consolidation of the Railway Properties of the United States into a Limited Number of Systems," 63 *ICC* 522, August 1921.

3. I.L. Sharfman, *The Interstate Commerce Commission, A Study in Administrative Law and Procedure*, The Commonwealth Fund, 1931; and I.L. Sharfman, *The Interstate Commerce Commission* (London: Oxford University Press, 1936).

4. Harold G. Moulton, "Fundamentals of a National Transportation Policy," *American Economic Review*, March 1934.

5. C.S. Duncan, *A National Transportation Policy*, Association of American Railroads, 1936.

6. *A National Transportation Program*, Transportation Association of America (2 volumes), 1938.

7. Warren H. Wagner, *A Legislative History of the Motor Carrier Act, 1935* (Denton, Maryland: ROE Publishing Company, 1935); and J.J. George, "The Federal Motor Carrier Act of 1935," *Cornell Law Quarterly*, Vol. 2, February 1936.

8. Fred D. Fagg, "National Transportation Policy and Aviation," *Journal of Air, Law*, April 1936.

9. D.P. Locklin, "Regulation of Water Carriers by the Interstate Commerce Commission," *Yale Law Journal*, Vol. 50, February 1941.

10. Ralph L. Dewey, "Transportation Act of 1940," *American Economic Review*, March 1941; and Kenneth F. Burgess, *Appraisal of Congressional Transportation Policies*, Institute of Transportation, New York University, 1944.

11. Charles D. Drayton, *Transportation Under Two Masters* (Washington, D.C.: National Law Book Company, 1946).

12. *Report on National Transportation Policy*, Chamber of Commerce of United States, April 30, 1946; and Anthony G. Allison, *A Plan to Revitalize the National Transportation Policy*, Transportation Association of America, 1947.

13. John S. Worley, *Our National Transportation Policy* (Ann Arbor, Michigan: Edwards Brothers Inc.), October 1945.

14. *A Report to the Congress by the Commission on Organization of the Executive Branch of the Government*, The Commission on Organization of the Executive Branch of the Government, March 1955.

15. Truman C. Bigham and Merrill J. Roberts, *Transportation* (New York: McGraw-Hill Book Company, Inc., 1946).

16. John H. Frederick, *Commercial Air Transportation* (Chicago: Richard D. Irwin, Inc., 1951); Charles A Taff, *Commercial Motor Transportation* (Homewood, Illinois: Richard D. Irwin, Inc., 1955); and James C. Nelson, *Railroad Transportation and Public Policy* (Washington, D.C.: The Brookings Institution, 1959).

17. For instance, see John H. Frederick, "National Transportation Policy: A Critical Analysis, *National Defense Transportation Journal*, March-April 1953.

18. *Statement of Policy*, American Waterways Operators, Inc., 1951; *Report by Cooperative Project on National Transportation Policy*, Transportation Association of America, May 1952; and *Blueprint for a New National Transportation Policy*, Federation for Railway Progress, 1953.

19. W.N. Leonard, *Railroad Consolidation Under the Transportation Act of 1920* (New York: Columbia University Press, 1946); and Merrill J. Roberts, "The Motor Transportation Revolution," *The Business History Review*, March 1956.

20. Kenneth U. Flood, *Advanced Traffic Management* (Dubuque, Iowa: W.C. Brown Company, 1959).

21. Paul W. Cherington, *Airline Price Policy* (Boston: The Plimpton Press, 1958); and J.R. Meyer, et al., *The Economics of Competition in the Transportation Industries* (Cambridge, Massachusetts: Harvard University Press, 1959).

22. *Revision of National Transportation Policy*, A Report to the President prepared by the Presidential Advisory Committee on Transport Policy and Organization, April 1955.

23. *Report on Reorganization of Federal Regulatory Agencies*, Landis Committee Report to President-Elect Kennedy, December 27, 1960.

24. Roy J. Sampson, *Obstacles to Railroad Unification* (Eugene, Oregon: Bureau of Business Research, University of Oregon, 1960).

25. Sidney L. Miller, Jr., "Federal Regulation of Transportation—A Case of Institutional Frustration," *Transportation Journal*, Winter 1961.

26. Maurice P. Arth, "Federal Transport Regulatory Policy," *American Economic Review*, May 1962.

27. Richard E. Caves, *Air Transport and Its Regulators* (Cambridge, Massachusetts: Harvard University Press, 1962).

28. For example, Dudley Pegrum, *Transportation Economics and Public Policy* (Homewood, Illinois: Richard D. Irwin, Inc., 1963).

29. Ann L. Friedlaender, *The Dilemma of Freight Transportation Regulation* (Washington, D.C.: The Brookings Institution, 1969).

30. Robert C. Fellmeth, *The Interstate Commerce Commission*, Ralph Nader's Study Group Report on the Interstate Commerce Commission and Transportation (New York: Grossman Publishers, 1970).

31. *A New Regulatory Framework, Report on Selected Independent Regulatory Agencies*, The President's Advisory Council on Executive Organization, 1971.

32. In 1971 a report summarized much of the regulatory criticism of recent studies. See James C. Nelson, *A Critique of Government Intervention in Transport*, Proceedings of a Conference on Regional Transportation Planning, Rand Corporation, Santa Monica, California, May 1971.

33. Marvin L. Fair, *Economic Considerations in the Administration of the Interstate Commerce Act* (Cambridge, Maryland: Cornell Maritime Press, 1972).

34. Thomas Gale Moore, Freight Transportation Regulation, *Surface Freight and the Interstate Commerce Commission* (Washington, D.C.: American Enterprise Institute), November 1972.

35. For example, Alan K. McAdams, "Do We Know What to Expect from Relaxation of Surface Transportation?" *Transportation Research Forum Proceedings*, November 1973; James W. McKee, *The Ends and Means of Regulation* (Washington, D.C.: The Brookings Institution, 1974); John C. Spychalski, "Criticisms of Regulated Freight Transport: Do Economists' Perceptions Conform with Institutional Realities?", *Transportation Journal*, 1975; and James C. Johnson and Donald V. Harper, "The Potential Consequences of Deregulation of Transportation," Land Economics, Spring 1975.

36. Two examples are, J.C. Nelson, *Implications of Evolving Entry and Licensing Policies in Road Freight Transport*, Proceedings of the International Conference on Transportation Research, First Conference, Bruges, Belgium, June 1973; and Victoria Ann Dailey, *The Certificate Effect: The Impact of Federal Entry Controls on the Growth of the Motor Carrier Firm*, Ph.D. dissertation, University of Virginia, June 1973.

37. Harvey M. Romoff, "The Deregulation of Transportation Rates—The Canadian Experience," *The Railway Management Review*, Volume 72, 1972.

38. Interstate Commerce Commission, *The Regulatory Issues of Today*, January 1975; and Interstate Commerce Commission, *ICC Internal Staff Recommendations for Improvement and Reform of the Commission's Operations*, July 7, 1975.

39. Interstate Commerce Commission, *A Cost and Benefit Evaluation of Surface Transport Regulation*, ICC Staff Report, Bureau of Economics, November 1976.

40. *Regulatory Reform: Report of the CAB Special Staff*, Civil Aeronautics Board, July 1975.

41. *The Regulated Ocean Shipping Industry*, U.S. Department of Justice, January 1977.

42. *Toward More Balanced Transportation: New Government Proposals*, Advisory Commission on Intergovernmental Relations, December 1974.

43. *U.S. Transportation—A Summary Appraisal*, Mitre Corporation, July 1975.

44. *Transport Review, Trends and Selected Issues*, Canadian Transport Commission, Ottawa, Canada, February 1977.

45. For instance, see A.P. Davis, Jr., "Public Interest Considerations in Transport Policy," *Proceedings–Transportation Research Forum*, 1973; and Grant M. Davis and Jack J. Holder, Jr., "Does the United States Have a Cohesive National Transportation Policy?–An Analysis," *Interstate Commerce Commission Practitioner's Journal*, March-April 1974.

3

Transportation Issues within an Evaluation Framework

A major contribution of the aggregation of historic transportation studies referenced in Chapter 2 was the identification of significant issues facing transportation policymakers throughout the history of federal involvement in transportation. Each study initially posed certain questions, or identified problems (issues), whose viability provided the rationale for the attempted research in the first place. In some cases, questions addressed remained unanswered, even after subsequent research and analysis. Thus, issue identification has traditionally been a major source of difficulty and contention of transportation policy research.

According to the dictionary, an issue is "a matter that is in dispute between two or more parties: a point of debate or controversy."[1] From a precise technical viewpoint, almost all, if not all, matters are issues because of their accompanying divergence of opinion. Even the most popular laws and programs are not without their critics as the transportation arena is comprised of competing carriers, and a host of interest groups with contrasting objectives. Controversy arises for many reasons, but most probably because of conflicts in goals, needs, and/or perspective among affected parties.

While issues can be clustered to reflect basic similarities and differences, effective analytical examination is not feasible without a comprehensive evaluation framework. The purpose of this chapter is to design such a framework so that historic and contemporary research issues can be analyzed against a set of institutional criteria—that is, significant organizational and institutional factors affecting the efficiency and effectiveness of both research and decision-making. This chapter initially identifies three ubiquitous problems inherent in our mixed public-private system of transportation planning, development, and operation. Then, a classification system based largely on these problems and logical administrative procedures is designed within which all issues can be placed and interrelationships among issues identified. Finally, historic and contemporary issues identified in past, including more recent, studies are evaluated within the parameters of the classification system.

Ubiquitous Problems

In the interrelated areas of conducting research and formulating public policy toward transportation, three broad factors have a substantial effect on issue identification, analysis, recommendations, and decision-making. These factors are referenced herein as ubiquitous problems because of their widespread existence, and their propensity to cause controversy and uncertainty in both research and policymaking. Ubiquitous problems are: (1) conflicts between national and regional interest, (2) discrepancies caused by the blend of public and private investment, and (3) measurement difficulties of externalities. It is imperative to effective analysis that researchers understand these conditions prior to undertaking research so that conclusions are not merely restatements of ubiquitous problems. Likewise, public policymakers should have similar knowledge in order to avoid the pitfalls of decision-making based on oversimplification of market conditions. In essence, realization of the three ubiquitous problems provides the underlayment for effective identification of major transportation issues, and development of an organizational framework for ensuing analysis.

National Versus Regional Interest

Research studies discussed in Chapter 2 assumed a need for national transportation policy, apparently based on the logic that public policy exists, whether explicit or implicit, in written form or not, and regardless of the degree of statement vagueness. Yet, these studies ignored the ubiquitous problem of national versus regional needs—a problem whose understanding is vital to the formulation of a rational position as to the need for comprehensive national policy in the first place.

Federal, state, and local governments all invest monies in transportation, with significant federal expenditures supporting state and local programs. For example, federal payments for highways (except on federally owned land) pass through the states, and federal funding of mass transit is filtered through both state and local public agencies. A classic example of the mixture of public funds in a single transportation problem is the funding of commuter rail service in Philadelphia. Managed by the Southeastern Pennsylvania Transportation Authority (SEPTA), the commuter system receives monies from two distinct federal programs—Section 5 operating subsidies as authorized by the Urban Mass Transportation (UMT) Act of 1964, as amended, and largely determined by the Delaware Valley Regional Planning Commission, and Section 17 emergency funding as legislated by the Regional Rail Reorganizational Act of 1973, financed through Section 17 of the UMT Act, in accordance with standards developed by the Rail Services Planning Office of the ICC. Furthermore, SEPTA receives aid from the Commonwealth of Pennsylvania, Department of Transportation, the City of Philadelphia, and four counties receiving rail commuter service. While state and local governments allocate their funds in accordance with their own criteria, the federal government often dictates conditions under which its funds may be used. In the case of SEPTA, two federal aid programs mean two different sets of criteria. Since federal, state, and/or local funds are mixed in many transit, as well as highway and other transportation ventures, it is difficult, if not impossible, to apply effective varying criteria to expenditures for the same project. Almost invariably, federal criteria are complied with, inasmuch as to ignore such standards may mean the loss of federal aid.

In practice, the imposition of federal conditions or criteria for the receipt and expenditure by state and local governments of federal funds has had three main objectives: (1) to limit the possibilities of corruption in the uses of the funds, (2) to specify the types of projects on which funds could be spent (for example, interstate, primary, secondary highways), and (3) to force local or regional governments "continuously and comprehensively" to plan their expenditures on transportation; regional planning commissions are instrumental here. In recent years a fourth objective has emerged—to assure that planning considers the views of local communities.

The federal government often specifies the types of projects it desires state and local governments to undertake by varying the amount of available federal funding. In some specific areas, competition for funds exists in the same marketplace—witness shifts from capital grants to operating subsidies for transit operations, or the battle between highway financing and transit funding. Also, government has been successful in preventing diversion of its funds to unauthorized uses. Thus, states and local governments appear sometimes to make decisions more related to the availability of federal funds than to the character of need for a particular facility. Solution of a transportation problem by means of a link in the interstate highway system continues to draw for state and local governments the largest share (90 percent) of federal funds. Even so, this alternative has sometimes been rejected. Thus, the effect of earmarking federal funds for specific types of projects appears to have induced some local areas to adopt transportation systems not necessarily best suited to their settlement patterns, economic bases, and/or community values.

One benefit of federal funding contrary to the above potential misallocation is that the requisite for involving local civic groups in transportation planning and decision-making has helped alleviate unwanted transportation projects. On the other hand, critics of local planning claim that plans are largely ignored and undertaken mainly to comply with federal requirements. In essence, the federal requirement of continuous and comprehensive local planning has had mixed results. Its usefulness and application was greatly limited by the federal fund earmarking process. Certainly, the magnitude of research studies were aided by additional funds, but sometimes the "best" solution to identified transportation problems was an interstate highway simply because it constituted the least drain on local resources.

A view strongly held at the state and local level is that the federal government ought to provide block grants to state and local governments for transportation purposes. The government would then be free to decide on fund allocation. The basic argument supporting block grants is that a national agency cannot absolutely identify local needs and apply national standards across regions having varying needs. If block grants were awarded, there would seemingly be less need for detailed project criteria. The argument against such grants implicitly rests on the belief that local governments are not able to make allocation decisions in either the best interests of local communities or, probably more appropriately, in the national interest.

In conclusion, varying needs and desires of localities and regions are sometimes in conflict with broader national interest. Where local interest prevails, national policy is allegedly weakened, but in reality this depends on perspective. In either situation, national politicians would still need to decide the level of federal aid to be provided for transportation. Whether or not the transportation system can best be served by regional or national policy is a question which should be answered as a requisite to formulating national transportation policy. Assuming the need for national policy in all areas of transportation is a disservice to national goals and public interest. Ignoring the possibility that regional policy might be the best form of national policy undermines research and limits the options available to policymakers.

Public and Private Investment

In the belief that sound business standards, often associated with economic principles, should be adopted by public agencies, many transportation facilities and operations have been put into the hands of authorities or publicly chartered companies which would presumably act like private companies. For instance, at state and local levels such agencies are proprietors of turnpikes, bridges, tunnels, ports, airports, and transit systems (for example, SEPTA). At the federal level they include the Alaska Railroad and the National Rail Passenger Service Corporation (AMTRAK). The question of standards and criteria is more or less regarded as irrelevant in the case of those authorities and public companies that more than cover operating expenses so as to provide a base for borrowing. While return to equity is not a factor, these public agencies meet the general private market criteria of expense coverage plus recovery of capital; they do not, nor are they intended, to meet the economic goal of profit organization. Turnpike, bridge, and tunnel authorities have been viable; the New York Port Authority has always been self-sufficient, and many airports are either self-supporting or close to it. However, public transit and surface travel generally do not recover operating expenses from riders, and very few are able to provide for capital needs. Scores of private transit lines have been converted to public systems in the past decade, and the publicly funded AMTRAK was created to provide subsidized intercity rail travel.

Transit systems and **AMTRAK** receive federal funds from general revenues to the Treasury. In 1975, Congress required **AMTRAK** to establish economic, social, and environmental criteria to determine whether particular routes in the **AMTRAK** system should be dropped or new routes added. Also in 1975, the Urban Mass Transportation Administration (**UMTA**) in DOT announced that thereafter state and local applicants for capital grants for mass transit would be required to carry out evaluations involving study of alternative ways of achieving their mass transportation objectives. Obviously, economic efficiency for the entire system is not the transportation objective in the cases of rail travel or transit systems.

Several major questions arise with respect to the proposition that user charges equal costs: Should a discount rate be applied to future streams of benefits expected to flow from current outlays? If so, what rate? And, is the public agency confronted with real competition? The private marketplace reflects the conditions of scarce resources, where output is limited, and society (as well as individuals) place a higher value on benefits derived from immediate resource use than from future use. Discounting, by weighing the worth of immediate returns against future returns, and providing rewards for waiting (interest and dividends), is the private market's means of deciding how much of society's resources, both public and private, will be used for both current and future output.

When public resources are used to obtain future benefits, an implicit assumption is that such future benefits will accrue. The difference in magnitude between future and current benefits, if both could be calculated, would represent society's reward for waiting. The inverse of the reward (that is, the amount by which future benefits are worth less than present benefits) is the discount rate which society has implicitly imposed. The less the public concern about waiting for benefits, the lower the discount rate. The greater the propensity to presently consume (that is, use the funded facilities before they are paid, rather than waiting), the higher the discount rate. Using highways as an example, the size of the discount rate governs how much of highway funds go into maintenance and how much into new construction.

Advocates of applying discount rates in public funding often contend that society's scarce resources are not wisely used unless public uses are subjected to the same disciplines as in the private sector. On the other hand, society may be more willing to provide for the future than would individuals—public education is an example. Thus, society's discount rate could be lower than private rates as expressed in interest rates and dividend yields. In general, there appears to be agreement among advocates of a public discount rate that social rates should be higher when private rates are higher, and vice versa.

In transportation, the problem of applying a discount rate to users of facilities financed by public funds appears to be acute, because much public and private funds are jointed in a single market area. Traditionally, significant and varying levels of federal aid have been provided to railroads, highways, waterways, and airports. Also, privately supported modes such as pipelines and railroads (assuming land grants were repaid by government-reduced railroad rates) compete with publicly supported waterways. How public discount rates could be established in such joint public-private environments is dubious at best. Yet, to do otherwise causes public expenditures to be economically less productive than private funds.

In regard to the matter of competition, the public section analogy with private enterprise rests on the proposition that public agencies will respond to the same economic stimuli and will have the same motivations as private companies. However, this includes the disposition toward competitive freedom. In fact, most public authorities operate in environments where competition is very limited, especially authorities managing bridges, tunnels, turnpikes, etc. To the extent that these public agencies are permitted to retain all of the proceeds they take in in the form of tolls and other charges, and in turn spend them on projects of their own choosing, their marginal dollars may be spent on projects which produce very low levels of return. Precautions which governments may take, but often do not, to assure that authorities spend their revenues wisely, is to require that all projects be subjected to some minimum discount rate. If no projects promise to produce positive net benefits, then either tolls should be reduced or unused net revenues should be turned over to authorities' governmental sponsors. That is to say, this should be done if the private analogy is to be honored. This proposition is dubious in the present system of allocating federal funds.

In conclusion, the lack of economic criteria (essentially a discount rate) for public funding of various transportation projects, generates a degree of chaos in the research and public-policy environment. No orderly system of evaluation exists because no explicit criteria have been proffered or stated. This condition exists among (across) public-investment programs, or within a single program. Thus, virtually hundreds of issues can emerge from this deficiency—a void which has resulted in attempts to quantify social goals and realizations—an improbable task at best.

Externalities

Economists refer to benefits which are not paid for by users, and outlays which are not borne by service-providing entities, as externalities. Encouragement of economic development may be a benefit to the entire community which is paid for by users; traffic congestion, city blight, and air pollution are a few examples of costs not paid by service providers. Projects may be justified because they create external benefit even if operating costs are not realized. In fact, much of our transportation system has been justified on this basis. Public funds spent on transit, rail passenger service, waterways, highways, airports and airways, and research, are examples of such projects.

Decisions as to whether public benefits are large enough to justify public expenditures are made by the political process. It appears that many politicians shy away from the application of funding standards because the cost of federal money to their constitutents is only that portion of federal tax that these constituents pay; this figure may be less than the benefits generated by a transportation project, although total benefits matched against total outlays may produce a negative result (that is, a return to the problem of regional versus national interest). One might assume that each member of Congress would checkmate every other member in pursuit of more than his pro-rata share of federal funds, but politics does not necessarily work that way. Some members are more powerful than others.

Basically, standards and criteria should help to determine the worthiness of projects, as well as their relative values. One method to achieve this goal is cost-benefit analysis, where calculated benefits and costs are placed in a single time frame by applying discount rates to both. Presumably, if the discount rate has been properly established, all projects showing discounted benefits equal to or exceeding costs would be worth consideration. Those with the highest benefit-cost ratios could be selected on a priority basis.

Benefit-cost analysis provides a formal apparatus for project evaluation. It begs the question, however, as to how benefits and costs are calculated. Once departure from the marketplace occurs, benefits and costs become matters of social preference subject to enormous variation over time. Literally, a person's, or a community's, benefit may be another's cost. This problem becomes more acute as benefits and costs are less determined by the market. When social and environmental factors are considered, benefit-cost analysis lends a spurious accuracy to a process which cannot be so finely determined. The standard that discounted benefits must exceed discounted costs simply breaks down before the ineluctable fact that benefits themselves, and costs, are matters of subjective determination which will vary among individuals and communities.

Classification System for Study Analysis

Without a system of classifying issues, problem identification and ensuing analysis is an exercise in semantics rather than substance. For example, a major issue to a lawmaker may be the proposed economic deregulation (entry, rates, mergers, etc.) of the airline industry. But what is described as the conflict of regulation versus deregulation to a congressional representative may be efficiency versus income distribution to an economist; stability versus higher rates to a shipper; control versus protection and stability to the airline industry; service versus lack of service to a rural resident; and, the fundamental question of the role of government to a political scientist. In fact, whether or not the federal government should play a role in planning, organizing, controlling, and/ or financing transportation is so controversial that a number of major issues are integral components of this broad question.

Figure 3-1 presents the environment depicting the role of government in the nation's transportation system. The transportation environment might best be described as a mixed economy where economic efficiency is but one of a number of considerations in public planning and decision-making. For those who do not favor federal intervention in transportation, there is no need for policy study. For those who perceive the need of government intervention, subsequent issues relate to the whys, wheres, when, for whom, and hows of federal promotion and control. As indicated in figure 3-1, the organizational structure of government (including the matter of federal-state-local responsibility), its financial commitment by scope and level, and its methods of implementing programs (taxes, block grants, ownership, etc.) are major matters imbedded with highly publicized controversy. Conceptually, decisions in these areas should be made by trading off incremental costs above the efficient level of output against a host of social-political considerations—namely, national defense, energy conservation, environmental protection, safety, and equity (income distribution, and "equal" treatment). In reality, political considerations and measurement uncertainties impede theoretical criteria.

Because of comprehensive government involvement in transportation, one procedure for classifying issues would be to separate the role of government between promotion and regulation, and to identify each issue as falling under either of these, or under more specifically segmented categories. This has been a popular approach of several past studies, a number of which have concluded that major issues arise because of conflicting goals of regulation (control) and promotion.[2] While there is significant validity to this common approach and understandable (logical) conclusion, it suffers from certain deficiencies as a basis for developing sound national transportation policy. First, it assumes the major involvement of federal promotion and regulation of transportation, both in areas of economics and safety. Such participation may be dubious in either the general area of regulation and promotion, or in specific modal or functional areas. Second, the approach is preoccupied with government organization, rather than focusing on needs which must be attended to by government, regardless of organizational structure. Third, it avoids addressing issues from the user's perspective, thereby failing to acknowledge that as a derived demand the movement of people and product evolves from societal living standards. Finally, it fails to define specifically the term "issue," thereby infusing semantical confusion among controversial matters such as goals, strategies, tools, impacts, and attitudes.

Correction of some of the above deficiencies was attempted in a few relatively recent studies, but in limited fashion. The 1961 *Doyle Report* cut across

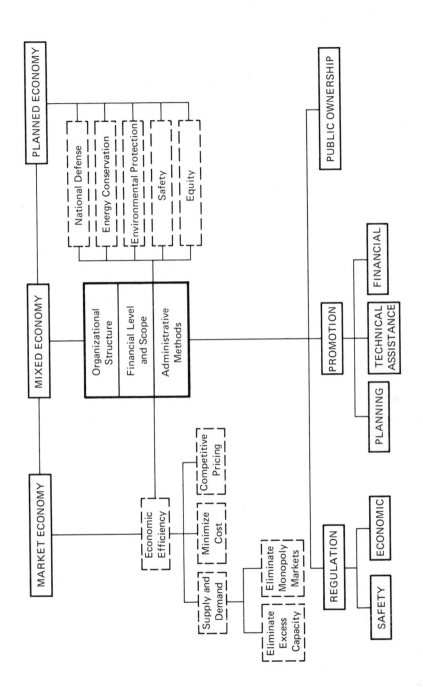

Figure 3-1. Transportation Research and Policymaking Environment: The Role of Government

modal lines but avoided the subject of issue relationships. Still, this study is among the most sophisticated ever completed on national transportation policy, and while void of emphasis on such current concerns as energy and environmental impact, many of the identified issues, subsequent analysis, and even recommendations, appear to be applicable to the contemporary environment. More recently, DOT's *Trends and Choices* mainly addressed problems expected to the year 2000. This study probably comes closest of all previous works to interrelating components of the transportation system, but by DOT's own admission the study was limited to revealing "the facts on transportation and . . . what the system will probably look like in 1990 under present policies and tendencies." Finally, and most recently, the *Magnuson Report* identified national transportation policy issues, but for the most part such issues were organized by mode of carriage.

In regard to an organized system of issues, the subjects addressed by studies referenced in Chapter 2 fell within three broad issue categories: *decision* (position and responsibility), *impact* (measurement and assessment), and *goal* (regional and national perspective). Each of these three categories is discussed below, and examples of applicable issues are identified. It is emphasized that the three categories of issues are by no means mutually exclusive, as they are interdependent and multifaceted.

Decision Issues

Issues directly related to the decision-making process are those relatively well-publicized controversies requiring some authoritative party to make a decision. These issues are two-dimensional in that their resolution requires, first, the determination of who is the responsibile party, and second, a decision (sometimes only positive or negative) to act by that party. For instance, the controversy over the 55-mile-per-hour (MPH) speed limit is a decision issue. While each state has adopted this speed limit, it has done so at the request, rather than at the order, of the federal government. Resolution (in terms of action, but not necessarily controversy) of the specific issue—Should the 55 MPH limit be a national standard?—requires a determination as to whether the federal government has the authority to institute a national speed standard and, if so (even after legislative change, or judicial conclusion), an affirmative or negative action by the government.

Decision issues tend to take functional titles so that they can be quickly identified by interested parties. Examples of such shortened titles and corresponding, popularly identified decision issues are listed in Table 3-1.

Table 3-1 is far from exhaustive as it simply is comprised of ten contemporary decision issues. These issues tend to be modally oriented, often because they are raised by carriers themselves. Also the government itself aides

Table 3–1
Examples of Decision Issues

Functional Title	Decision Issue
User charges	Should inland water carriers be forced to pay a user charge (tax, lock fee, segment fee, etc.) for their use of waterways maintained by the U.S. government?
Regulatory constraints	What regulatory legislation and/or criteria inhibit(s) the efficient flow of people and goods?
Coal slurry pipelines	Should government aid in the development and implementation of coal slurry pipelines by promoting the availability of land and water?
AMTRAK	Should government continue to finance intercity rail passenger service?
Motor carrier weight and size standards	Are national standards desirable for limiting the size of motor carriers, weight of shipment, and use of double and triple trailers?
Deregulation	Should interstate motor carriage and airline service be economically deregulated?
Transit financing	Is it socially desirable to finance urban transit systems with funds from nonuser taxes?
Highway Trust Fund	Should the Highway Trust Fund be maintained? Should funds from this fund be used to maintain the present Interstate System? Is it desirable to use trust funds for nonhighway (such as transit) projects?
Pricing	Should regulatory pricing policy be cost-related or based on value of service (demand-sensitive)?
Light-density lines	Should railroads be permitted to abandon light-density lines? If not, should the lines be subsidized? By which level of government? Should coal lines be banked for futher use?

modal fragmentation inasmuch as the U.S. Department of Transportation is structured along modal lines. Still, decision issues can bebroadened to include all modes for sake of conceptual, but not necessarily practical, consistency. For instance, the user charge issue (inland waterways) can be extended to all modes, but motor carriers, buses, airlines, and automobiles already pay user fees, and the railroads own their own rights-of-way. On the other hand, the question of AMTRAK subsidies can be extended to inland waterway users (notice the similarity of the user charge and AMTRAK issues), urban public transit riders, rural residents and/or shippers, handicapped and elderly travelers, etc. More obviously, the issue of airline deregulation applies to motor carriers and railroads, although varying operating characteristics of each mode affect subsequent analysis and possible conclusions.

Finally, it is noted that decision issues often go beyond decision-making at simply the positive-negative level. The question of the 55 MPH speed limit only requires a yes-or-no response when it is phrased at the specific figure of 55 MPH, but the question can also be phrased as: What should be the maximum travel speed on our major highways? This is no different from asking the 55 MPH question in concert with similar questions at MPH's of 50, 51, 52, etc. Thus, decisions relate to both action and responsibility, and such decision-making is often two-staged—for example, affirmative or negaitve response, and specific method of implementation.

Shown in figure 3-2 below, in outline form, is the relationship among a decision issue and its two major components: attitude and implementation. It is important to note that decision issues often appear to remain unresolved because of controversy over authority and method of implementation. Thus, while many individuals (quite probably the majority) may favor the 55 MPH speed limit, a national standard may be undermined by the controversy over whether the federal government has the Constitutional authority to set such a standard. Also, since states enforce speed limits on most highways, questions arise as to the source of funding speed-limit monitoring. Likewise, the adoption of waterway user charges may be adversely affected by the administrative problems and cost of developing and operating a fee-collection system. And finally, many public urban transit systems allocate their operating deficits to serviced communities, rather than revenues and costs separately, because of difficulties in stimulating local jurisdictions to agree on methods of implementation. In conclusion, decision issues are often well publicized and popularly entitled, but they do not address the core (root) faucets of transportation controversy. Rather, their resolution results in implementation of national transportation policy, but such resolution depends on answers to much deeper questions—especially questions of economic, social, and geographic impact.

Impact Issues

While decision issues are often (or should be) resolved after careful analysis of expected impact, in both cost effectiveness and cost-benefit analyses, measure-

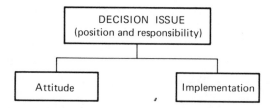

Figure 3-2. Segmentation of Decision Issues

ment and interpretation of impact are hotly contested issues. Controversy abounds because of the difficulty of identifying the supply (cost) side of transportation where joint and especially common costs are so prevalent, the lack of a homogeneous measure of demand demonstrated by the deficiencies of the passenger-mile (also extremely difficult and costly to measure) and ton-mile variables, and the preponderance of social and environmental factors where qualified judgment is substituted for quantifiable measures.

Impact controversies are demonstrated by the decision issue of (motor carrier) deregulation. Questions currently being discussed are impacts from proposed deregulation on service to rural communities, concentration of carriers within the motor-carrier industry, level of rates, industrial location, development of private carriage, operational safety, environmental factors, and conservation of energy. The resolution of impact issues depends upon two component issues: the interrelationships within the transportation network, and the availability, measurement, and reliability of data. For instance, whether motor-carrier economic deregulation results in a higher or lower level of rates primarily depends on the nature of trucking costs (economies of scale) and price elasticity of demand. Yet the question of scale economies has historically been controversial, and price elasticity may be different for each of the millions (combinations of origins and destinations) of markets, is constantly in a dynamic state, and cannot be separated from other elasticities (income, service, etc.) with any reliable degree of assurance. Thus, impact issues can be viewed as having two subcomponents, as shown in the schematic outline in figure 3-3 below.

Above relationships are evidenced by the recent controversy over energy conservation. One impact issue may be stated as: What effect on energy consumpton will result from allowing conglomerates to practice intercorporate hauling within their own family of companies? To address this issue properly a host of secondary impact issues relating to market structure also need to be studied, including: (1) the amount of cross-hauling currently existing among major corporations who have, or are candidates for, private carriage; (2) methods

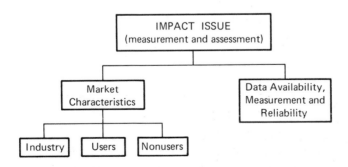

Figure 3-3. Segmentation of Impact Issues

by which potential cross-haul traffic currently moves; (3) cost and fuel use of such traffic; (4) empty-return miles by size and type of vehicle; (5) potential mileage savings by cross-hauling; (6) cost difference if cross-hauling is permitted; and (7) effect on currently used carriers. Furthermore, many questions relating to user and nonuser costs, benefits, and appropriate financing shares are entwined in impact evaluation. Again, the resolution of issues relating to industry characteristics largely depends on data availability and reliability. For years, intercity freight analysis has been limited because the ICC does not collect and publish data on motor-carrier traffic flows; a 1 percent sample of state-to-state flows is available for railroads. Also, the transit industry has faced barriers in conducting research and allocating operating deficits because of difficulty (including the high cost) in accurately calculating passenger-miles. And finally, the aggregate output measure of freight transportation, the ton-mile, is sufficiently controversial to restrict studies on productivity, comparative carrier efficiency, and fuel conservation.

It is a rather obvious conclusion of those familiar with the transportation literature that matters of industry characteristics and related data consume the overwhelming portion of study by transportation planners, economists, systems analysts, accountants, and others. Some such subjects of controversy are:

cost finding

price elasticity of demand

economies of scale

modal shares

demand forecasting

rate level and structure

profit determination

industry structure

productivity measurement

managerial effectiveness

determination of ownership

traffic flows

cost of capital

vehicle capacity and utilization

accounting methods

evaluation of social benefits

Analyses of the above, and of other similar subjects, tend to be of a technical nature, thus sometimes causing communication gaps among various parties interested in the resolution of transportation issues. While technicians arrive at certain conclusions based on impact analysis, even where consensus is achieved they may be in disagreement with policy decision-makers who adopt broader and sometimes different criteria for determining and implementing transportation policy. Thus, issues relating to transportation goals are also of prime import.

Goal Issues

To the clinical, sometimes called "pure" economist, the basis for decision-making is economic efficiency—that is, the optimal allocation of resources. However, concern with supply equaling demand, minimizing cost, increasing productivity, eliminating excess capacity, and generally optimizing the factors of production (land, labor, capital, and ownership), is not the sole focus of public policymakers. Instead, they are also concerned with national defense, energy conservation, environmental protection (pollution, noise, blight), safety, and equity (income distribution and availability of service). The transportation system is characterized by many examples where economic efficiency was sacrificed in order to fulfill social and political goals—AMTRAK, St. Lawrence Seaway, urban transit, people movers, Northeast Corridor, commuter railroads, and feeder airline service.

Shown in figure 3-4 below, in schematic form, are the relationships among the components of goal issues. It is interesting to note that both the determination of which objectives are important enough to be considered, and the weights given to each goal in the so-called trade-off analysis, are somewhat dependent on geographic perspective. For instance, a supporter of urban transit may stress energy conservation and environmental impact over economic efficiency, while a rural resident may complain bitterly about his tax dollars subsidizing urban communities. Conversely, the rural resident may emphasize service equity in favoring continued truck and/or airline regulation if accompanied by cross-subsidization of rural markets, while urban residents may stress the economic waste of such service. Contradicitons of transportation objectives not only exist between urban and rural communities, but also between states and regions. For instance, uniformity of trucking size and weight restrictions does not exist among all states; also, twin trailers are permitted in some states while not in others. On a broader regional basis, some areas are vitally concerned with highway construction and maintenance (Southwest, Rocky Mountain area), and have virtually no need for urban rapid transit. Thus, the issue of using the Highway Trust Fund for rapid transit is controversial by regional standards.

Goal issues change over time and in accordance with environmental conditions and political climate. For instance, energy conservation has only recently

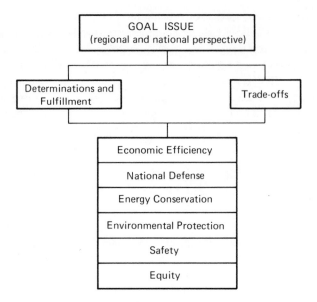

Figure 3-4. Segmentation of Goal Issues

come to the front as a major goal issue, and its significance will probably not be felt for another five years or so; much depends on world conditions (availability of foreign energy sources) and political decision-making (deregulation of natural gas industry). Economic efficiency became more of a secondary issue in the 1960s when the social revolution accelerated, but may return to strength if proponents of deregulation are successful. National defense currently receives minor consideration from transportation policymakers because of the maturity of our transportation system, while safety and environmental impact are presently the vogue.

Closing the Loop

All three classes of issues are interrelated, forming a closed-loop system of evaluating a subject. A prudent decision (decision issue) on any matter largely depends on anticipated impact (impact issue), and how one views that impact in relationship to goals and priorities (goal issue). On the other hand, an individual's assessment of concern and goals often depends on measurable impact, which in turn depends on the nature of the decision in question. The relationship of the three classes of issues is presented in table 3-2, where the example of waterway user charges is examined. The decision to consider waterway user charges is based on such industry characteristics as: (1) water carriers presently

Table 3–2
Three Levels of National Transportation Issues

Type of Issue	Major Components	Explanation	Example
I. Decision	A. Attitude B. Implementation	Well-publicized contro-versies requiring decision-making judgment by public policymakers	I. Waterway user charges A. Adoption or status quo B. Full tax versus segment fee
II. Impact	A. Industry charac-teristics B. Data availability, measurement, and reliability	Controversies of impact from decision issues on consumers, shippers, carriers, regions, etc.	II. Impact on various segments of in-land waterways A. Railroad versus water carrier costs B. Authenticity of water carrier oper-ating costs (not currently reported in detail to ICC)
III. Goal	A. Determinations and fulfillment B. Trade-off evalua-tions	Determination of trans-portation goals, strictly to fulfill goals, and evaluation of goal trade-offs	III. Regional interest versus national perspective A. Inclusion of fuel conservation as part of evaluation criteria B. Economic effi-ciency (eliminate subsidy) equity (other carriers pay for right-of-way) versus conserva-tion of fuel and income distribu-tion.

do not pay user fees, (2) the government subsidizes inland waterways, and (3) other carriers pay for right-of-way use. Yet, the emphasis given full consideration and equity within the trade-off analysis of objectives somewhat depends on industry structure—that is, the magnitude of fuel involved, and the fact that water carriers are important to the economic climate of specific regions. In this sense, while politicians support their attitudes toward user charges (including methods of revenue collection) relative to general objectives of economic efficiency, fuel conservation, equity, etc., these general attitudes and accompanying rationale of public interest should be supported with hard-core impact analysis. If a national transportation policy is to be developed, stated, and implemented, then the national system of transportation should be identified, examined, and understood.

The importance of impact issues is evidenced in figure 3–5, where knowledge of industry characteristics and adequate data are identified as key factors of issue identification, developing priorities for issue resolution, and analytical evaluation of identified issues. While the explicit intent of this study was to identify major transportation issues, and not their basis for resolution, the depth and importance of impact issues should be noted; such notation is contrary to popular identification of issues where functional titles (decision issues) are the rule.

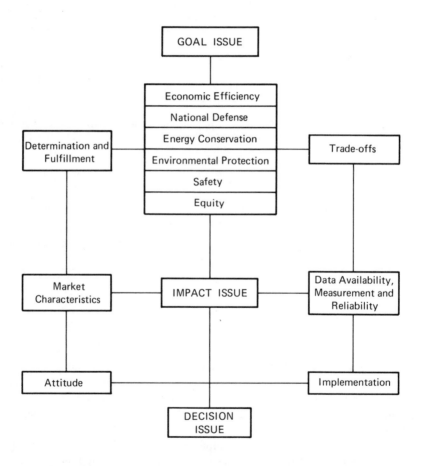

Figure 3–5. Relationships among Three Classes of Issues

Traditional Issues

Recognizing conflicting regional and national interests, lack of economic criteria in public decision-making, and the difficulties of measuring nonmarket benefits and costs, traditional studies of national transportation policy matter appear to have identified issues within a narrow and simplistic framework. Questions addressed have had little support, order, or placement within a broader evaluation framework. The *Coordinator's Reports* in the 1930s marked the beginning of comprehensive study of national transportation policy, and in ensuing decades many issues have remained unchanged; a few have been resolved; some have changed in intensity; and others have experienced a metamorphosis of form.

In identifying alleged significant issues of their eras, many past studies were overly broad and vague in their approaches, conclusions, and recommendations, thus reading like a civics textbook rather than a meaningful study having practical application. Even the *Coordinator's Reports* were vague in recommending that national transportation objectives be established, and that aid programs should be developed to meet such objectives. Many studies, as far back as the *Duncan* book in 1936, called for a national policy stressing coordination and equality, and efficient and adequate service. Another popular and obscure theme was that of striking a balance between competition and public control (National Resources Planning Board in 1942). Similarly the fulfillment of basic management principles such as establishing responsibility and accountability have been recommended by the *Hoover* reports and other organizational studies. The *Dearing-Owens* study in 1949 exemplified many conclusions in recommending that: (1) national policy should be based on sound economics, be unified, and be consistent; (2) regulatory policy should be coordinated. The *Sawyer Report* in 1949 went a little further in recommending that careful analysis of benefits be made prior to public investment in transportation—a statement somewhat in the same vein as the *Weeks Report*'s conclusion (1955) that all impediments to a financially strong common carrier system should be removed.

The second *Hoover Report* (1955) recognized vagueness in the policy statement and recommended that the policy be studied and revised by Congress to make it more definite and detailed; this was a promise emphasized by the *Doyle Report* in 1961, and affirmed in *Norton* in 1966. However, in the late 1960s and early 1970s attention turned to regulation (Friedlaender, Nader, Moore, Fair), and a number of studies addressed issues of regulatory need, constraints, and criteria. Currently, with newfound environmental and energy concerns affecting decision-making, the 1940 policy statement may again draw attention. This was not the focus of either *Trends and Choices* or the *Magnuson* study (both in 1977), but may be renewed by DOT itself through distribution of its so-called "Needs Studies" every two years.

Even in the more contemporary studies, issues identified and addressed seem to ignore the type of order exemplified by the classification system presented in this chapter. For instance, table 3-3 lists one transportation expert's hierarchy of major issues. "Planning" is the top vote-getter, but this rather vague managerial function is the kind of subject not requiring research to support its desirability. A more meaningful issue may be the question of who should have the responsibility for planning various phases and segments of our transportation infrastructure. Similarly, "Management" is also a priority issue identified in table 3-3, but the need for administrative expertise can be concluded on an ex-ante basis. The list of so-called problem areas in table 3-3 represents a conglomeration of decision, impact, and goal issues, as well as subjects of carrier need fulfillment.

Table 3-4 presents the ten most critical issues in transportation as identified by the Transportation Research Board in 1977. Again, the list represents a

Table 3-3
One Expert's View of Overall Transportation Industry Problems, 1972

Problem Areas	Issue	Severity[a] Ranking
Planning	Scope and sophistication	26
Management	Need for expertise	22
Rates	Relaxation of regulatory restrictions	22
Intermodal coordination	Methods of promotion	22
Labor	Antiquted work rules and settlement process	20
Technology	Need for incentives	20
Research and data	Level and concentration	19
Image	Quality of service	18
Structural cost inequities	User charges and rail track subsidies	17
Financial	Subsidization and abandonment	17
Marketing	Effectiveness	15
Environmental and ecological	Modal standards	13
Industry structure	Merger and cntry deregulation	7
Foreign competition	Policy, planning, and strategy	7

Source: John W. Drake, "Transportation Industry Problem Areas and Power Relationships," *Proceedings–Transportation Research Forum*, Volume XIII, Number 1, 1972.

[a]Ranking based on aggregate score of estimated severity by eleven industry areas, where range is from 0 (negative severity) to 3 (high severity). Thus, a possible total score of 33 (3 × 11) was possible for the following industry areas: railroad, trucking, automobile manufacturing, highways, urban, airlines, aviation infrastructure, maritime, pipeline, and military.

Table 3-4

The Ten Most Critical Issues in Transportation Identified by the Executive Committee, Transportation Research Board, 1977

1. Financial requirements and alternatives for transportation systems and services
2. Energy efficiency
3. Intergovernmental responsibility
4. Maintenance technology and management
5. Performance criteria and design standards
6. Effects of regulation
7. Improvement of existing nonurban transportation facilities
8. Transportation, land-use control, and city forms
9. Transportation and the environment
10. Safety

blending of all three types of issues structured in this book, with maximum concentration on goal and impact issues. Issues are not interrelated and a hierarchical structure is not suggested.

One of the more curious lists of issues is that presented by DOT in its *Trends and Choices* in 1977, as shown in table 3-5. Given three different scenarios, the emphasis of issues shifts from economic, to social, and finally to values. For instance, table 3-5 shows that under distress conditions, problems are the waste associated with excess capacity, regulatory constraints, inefficient automobiles, etc. However, if these problems are solved and the country moves to a "success" environment, attention will focus on social concerns such as traffic noise, congestion, air pollution, highway safety, and energy shortages. Obviously, transportation currently exists within both a partial distress and success framework. Finally, if economic and social problems are solved, values will shift back to small living units and issues such as inadequate research will evolve. Table 3-5 represents DOT's thinking on issue structure and relationships after a comprehensive policy study, but such a conceptual structure required no research and little, if any, analytical input.

Most recently, as presented in table 3-6, the *Magnuson* study analyzed transportation issues in the older, more traditional manner of classifying problems by mode of carriage. Freight issues were separated from passenger issues, and analysis was presented for railroads, motor carriers, airlines, water carriers, pipelines, and intermodal freight service. The report identified two major policy issues as the lack of coherent regulatory policy, and the need for improved funding criteria, tools of analysis, and organization—again, traditional concerns long recognized as existing, requiring little, if any, research to conclude.

Table 3-5

Major Transportation Issues to the Year 2000 Identified by the Department of Transportation, 1977

Scenarios		
Success	*Distress*	*Transformation*
(Traditional values successfully realized, resulting in growth and reduction of inefficiency)	(External causes adversely affect realization of traditional values)	(Shift away from traditional values to small-neighborhood planning and population dispersion)
Traffic noise	Overcapacity	Low level of federal research, development, and demonstration projects
Congestion	Unamortized cost	
Air pollution	Increasing carrier specialization	Cost and maintenance of autos with safety and antipollution devices
Highway safety	Regulatory constraints	
Shortage of liquid fuels	Urban sprawl	
	Inefficient auto pollution system	
	Increasing cost of auto maintenance	

Source: U.S. Department of Transportation, *National Transportation Trends and Choices (to the Year 2000)*, January 1977.

Within the cloudiness of historic transportation policy studies, a number of issues have intermittently, if not continually, resurfaced. Although not necessarily an all-inclusive list, these popular issues are identified and briefly discussed below.

Organizational Consolidation: The creation of a single promotional agency (DOT) was recommended for over thirty years before its realization, and almost every ensuing major policy study concluded that such an agency was needed. None of these studies recommended the exclusion of the Federal Maritime Administration which is currently in the Department of Commerce. No study addressed the issue of the rationale for such a long lead time between the many recommendations for a single agency and their implementation.

In recent years, some studies have recommended the consolidation of the ICC, CAB, and FMC into one agency (*Ash Report* in 1971 is a major example). This recommendation, as the DOT advocacy, is based on the qualified logic of eliminating duplicity and creating a balanced regulatory posture among the modes, rather than justified on calculated cost-benefit analysis. Regulatory

Table 3-6
Major Transportation Policy Issues as Identified by Senate
Committee on Commerce, Science, and Transportation, 1977

I. Major Policy Issues
    A. Lack of coherent regulatory policy (inconsistent treatment of modes)
    B. Need for improved funding criteria, tools of analysis, and organization
II. Freight Policy Issues
    A. Railroad
        1. Rail industry restructuring
            a. economies of scale
            b. rationalization of rail plant
        2. Federal funding of rehabilitations
        3. Electrification
        4. Light-density lines
        5. Rate regulations
    B. Motor Carrier
        1. Economic regulation
        2. Maximum vehicle weights and dimensions
    C. Air-economic regulation
    D. Water
        1. Improvements—funding
        2. User charges
    E. Pipeline—coal slurry pipelines
    F. Intermodal Freight Service
        1. Institutional restrictions
        2. Public benefits
III. Passenger Policy Issues
    A. Rail—level of service in public interest
    B. Auto
        1. Highway needs
        2. Use of Highway Trust Fund
    C. Air—deregulation
    D. Intermodal Passenger Service—role of government

reorganization continues to be studied by Congress and a series of reports on the subject were released in late 1977 and in 1978.[3]

Regulatory Reform: Recommendations for regulatory reform are simply an outgrowth of regulation. Once controls are initiated, enforcement criteria are naturally controversial. Reform ranges from changes in public standards for rate-setting, mergers, service abandonment, operating authority, equipment pooling, common ownership, etc., to complete economic deregulation of a particular transport mode. The *Coordinator's Reports* recommended strengthened regulation during a period when business instability was a prime concern. The *BIR Report* in 1942 affirmed many of the *Eastman* recommendations, and while the 1961 *Doyle Report* made a number of recommendations to liberalize regulatory constraints, it stopped short of promoting deregulation. It was not until the early 1970s that deregulation became the vogue. Ann Friedlaender's book in

1969, followed by Tom Moore's works quantifying the cost of regulation, began the push. Also, relatively high motor-carrier profits, combined with railroad bankruptcy, faced a conservative administration and thus the Nixon forces proposed deregulation of the motor-carrier industry, and soon thereafter, airline deregulation. The Carter administration is also on record as favoring at least some form of economic deregulation of airlines in particular, and of motor carriers to possibly a lesser extent. It does not appear that any major research study on national transportation resulted in conclusions favoring deregulation.

Waterway User Charges: Support for waterway user charges is a traditional conclusion and/or recommendation of prior studies. This position is taken in the *Coordinator's Reports*, the *BIR Report*, the *Dearing-Owens* study, the *Mueller Report*, and the *Doyle Report*. No major study reviewed recommends against user charges, although several did not address the issue. User charges on inland waterways appear to be a sound recommendation which has not been implemented because of regional interests' taking precedence over national interest.

Interpretation of Policy Statement: Ever since the statement on national transportation policy was written into the 1940 act, a number of research studies have focused on the vagueness of the statement. The *Doyle Report* was especially critical of certain phrases and recommended a refined version of the statement. At the heart of the matter is controversy over the definition of "inherent advantage," and whether or not all modes of transportation should be maintained, even if inefficiency results—that is, the contradiction between promoting efficiency and protecting the various modes.

Classification Voids

It should already be obvious to the reader that historic transportation policy studies are glutted with decision issues. What is not so obvious is that such saturation is at the expense of impact issues. Rather, discussion and analysis of various types of impacts emerge in adversary proceedings and congressional hearings where credibility is undermined by vested interests and acknowledged bias. The question naturally arises as to why impact measurement and evaluation is so often ignored in policy research studies. Three speculative answers come to mind. First, data deficiencies undermine the effectiveness of impact evaluations in many areas of transportation. In fact, there is practically no area of transportation where data are sufficient from a national perspective. This is especially true in areas requiring economic analysis. Freight traffic flows are limited to a controversial 1 percent sample (of waybills) for railroads, while similar information, inadequate as it is, is not available for other modes. Flow statistics from the Census of Transportation are somewhat helpful, but limited to manufactured products and aggregated in such a way as to hinder detailed evaluation. Transportation cost information is plentiful, but fraught with controversy, partially due to difficulties in calculating and assigning joint and common costs, and partially due to judgment required in allocating costs of an economic system (for example, transport mode) to political and/or geographic subdivisions. Furthermore, regulated carriers comprise only one segment of a much larger freight-carrying industry, and data on private and exempt carriage is extremely limited and not thought to be reliable. In the passenger area, data is readily available among some systems, but the all-important variable of passenger-miles is expensive to calculate and subject to definitional problems. Consequently, many historic projections of traffic growth, modal splits, price elasticity, ridership, and revenue need have been wide of the mark. In fact, transportation data is so questionable that a consensus has not been reached regarding an output measure of freight transportation; the ton-mile is the single factor most often adopted, but this measure has shortcomings for purposes of comparative analysis. The passenger-mile is generally accepted as the product of passenger transportation, but is both difficult and expensive to calculate accurately. In summary, transportation data is plentiful due to the sheer volume of passengers and products moving between hundreds and thousands of origins and destinations; however, huge voids in data are evident relative to evaluation needs, and reliability in many areas is dubious at best.

A second apparent reason for the shortage of impact analysis may be an unconscious fear of subsequent results. On one hand measured impact may show a particular group and/or geographic region being adversely affected by a proposed action, and such a conclusion would offend political supporters of parochialism. On the other hand impact analysis may reveal the probable consequences of a number of national transportation policies—that one party or region benefits at the expense of others. For instance, introduction of "missionary" (low rates to develop markets) freight rates to the Southwest may have accelerated industrial development of southern agricultural communities to the dismay of New Englanders. This thesis of avoiding overall sound programs because of specific unpleasantries is discussed in more detail in Chapter 5; it has been expounded by a leading national figure and set forth as a basic principle of our national public policy, entitled "do no direct harm."

A third possible reason for avoiding impact analysis may have to do with the major source of funding transportation policy studies—the federal government. All of the major comprehensive studies discussed in Chapter 2 (Cullom, Eastman, BIR, Hoover, Doyle, Magnuson, etc.) were financed by either Congress or an executive branch agency. This is not to accuse researchers of an unwillingness to "bite the hand that feeds them." Individuals' intentions, ethics, and standards are not known to this author and are beyond the scope of speculation. Rather, government studies have tended to ask the wrong questions so that even "good" and responsive answers result in obvious and somewhat irrelevant conclusions. Wrong questions are ones which do not consider the role of government in planning, organizing, and controlling the transportation system. Instead, they are questions which are mostly generated by carrier financial instability (e.g., bankrupt railroads, insolvent airlines, deficit transit operators, etc.) , and focus on alternative means of federal assistance to "solve" the problem. Alleged solutions usually are unified public programs, increased public expenditures, government reorganization, and/or establishment of clear national transportation policies. For instance, consider the recommendations of a recent study by the Senate Governmental Affairs Committee after a two-year research effort, and notice the similarity to prior federal transportation research:

The transfer of the civil waterway functions of the Army Corps of Engineers to DOT.

The transfer of ship operations and construction subsidies from the Commerce Department's Maritime Administration to DOT.

The shift of the Civil Aeronautics Board's local service airline subsidy program to DOT.

The combination of all water, air, highway, rail and mass transit grants and programs into a single transportation budget account under DOT.

The enactment of a National Transportation Policy Act, which would outline unified national goals and priorities, and give the Secretary of Transportation broad powers to propose regulations regarding any functions of the Interstate Commerce Commission, Civil Aeronautics Board and Federal Maritime Commission.[4]

Both in principle, and for most of the proposals, no differences exist among the above Senate report and the *Coordinator's Reports* during the 1930s and the *Doyle Report* in 1964, among others.

Deficiencies of historic research on national transportation policy are more elaborately discussed in Chapter 5. Still, it is important to note in this chapter that the federal government itself may be a cause of transportation research inadequacies because of its avoidance of the major root question (that is, the role of government) in favor of analyzing alternative public programs to aid transport carriers. Impact analyses required for such research often ignore users and geographic regions. Thus, impact issues take a distant back seat to traditional decision issues as the federal government perpetuates itself as the mainstay of the transportation industry. As discussed in the following chapter, federal involvement in transportation has continually increased throughout history and, in view of relatively recent acceleration, gives promise of eventually becoming the provider of much of the country's transportation service.

Finally, what may be most disturbing about the subject of issue classification is that past research efforts have not attempted to organize and interrelate alleged transportation problems. The lack of a systematic approach to research and analysis has resulted in communication problems and analytical differentiation based on semantics rather than substance. Determination of trade-offs among various goals cannot be undertaken unless all national objectives, contradictory as they may be, are identified and assigned relative priorities. Likewise, transportation policy decisions should not be made prior to impact analysis. To designate issues as "major" or "significant" because of the vociferousness of interest groups is contrary to the public interest. A classification scheme which locates issues within a comprehensive and interrelated network (that is, system) is prerequisite to meaningful transportation research and the development of effective national transportation policy.

Notes

1. *Webster's Seventh New Collegiate Dictionary*, G. & C. Merriam Company, Springfield, Massachusetts, 1970.
2. For example, *Issues Involved in a Unified and Coordinated Federal Program for Transportation*, Report to the President from the Secretary of Commerce, 1949; *The High Cost of Conflicting Public Transportation Policies*, Association of American Railroads, 1951; and *The Future of American Transportation*, The American Assembly, Columbia University, 1971.
3. For example, *Study on Federal Regulation, Volume V, Regulatory Organization*, Committee on Governmental Affairs, United States Senate, 95th Congress, 1st Session, December 1977.
4. Ibid.

4 Policy Overview

National transportation policy is exemplified by the aggregation of all federal legislation, judicial decisions, executive-branch programs, and applicable rhetoric affecting transportation. In this sense, "national transportation *policies*" is a more appropriate designation of federal involvement in transportation markets. Much has been written about each federal bill, proposed legislation, regulatory decision, subsidy criterion, safety standard, etc., and the task of evaluating each subject is not within the scope of this book. Rather, in order to relate transportation policy research to national transportation policy in general, a policy overview is required. This chapter is devoted to presenting such an overview by examining in broad fashion the scope, magnitude, and direction of federal aid (subsidies) and economic regulation (rates, entry, mergers, etc., as opposed to safety regulation) of interstate transportation.

Nature of Transportation Subsidies

Although an embedded cornerstone of our national transportation policy, "subsidy" is a misunderstood and often-abused term. In some cases subsidies are viewed in the narrow context of direct payments without identifying total costs to both user and nonuser of the subsidized facility. At other times, benefits are ignored. There is even a tendency on the part of many to exclude themselves as beneficiaries. Subsidy is defined as: (1) a grant or gift of money or other property, and (2) something intended to aid, support, or comfort. From the narrowest perspective transportation subsidies would be limited to receipt of direct cash payments from government. A somewhat broader interpretation comprehends subsidy as the remission of charges otherwise payable; in other words, the purchase of goods and services at prices above market value (subsidy to the vendor), or their sale at less than market value (subsidy to the purchaser). A still wider meaning identifies recipients of subsidy as all enterprises, including individuals, whose economic position is improved, or whose purposes are advanced, through the operation of forces instigated by government. This latter definition is preferred in transportation circles because it provides a basis for the most comprehensive measure of subsidies, and for subsequent comparison of public aid to all transport modes. Thus, transportation subsidies are benefits enjoyed in excess of those purchased in the marketplace, whether such benefits take the form of direct cash grants, or are indirectly received and partially concealed by a variety of institutions, practices, and programs.

Six forms of financial[1] subsidy have been cited authoritatively: (1) direct cash, (2) tax, (3) credit, (4) benefit-in-kind, (5) purchase, and (6) regulatory.[2] Cash payments are the most readily observed and measured form of subsidy. In its simplest form, cash payment is directly related to the activity subsidized and is delivered from government directly to the individual or corporate recipient. For instance, annual subsidy payments to airlines, as administered by the Civil Aeronautics Board, is in the form of cash disbursements. However, since payments such as those received by AMTRAK are not enjoyed by the National Rail Passenger Corporation itself (that is, they represent a pass-through benefit to rail passengers), these grants are designated as benefit-in-kind subsidies. In reality, both airline and rail passengers benefit from federal subsidies, but a key difference between the two examples above is that airline stockholders also benefit while AMTRAK is a public agency.

The second form of federal aid, tax subsidies, far exceeds direct cash payments to transportation entities, and is the largest of the federal noncash subventions, totaling $39.9 and $59.7 billion, or 62 and 63 percent of estimated total federal subsidies in 1970 and 1975, respectively.[3] The investment tax credit is one such form of tax subsidy, flowing only to those subject to income taxation. Another tax-subsidy provision exempts interest on state and local debt from federal income taxes. This subsidy is somewhat more difficult to quantify than investment tax credits since there is a disparity between subsidy cost to the federal government and value to the recipients; that is, the federal government can estimate the amount of tax receipts foregone from this policy, but it is somewhat more difficult to ascertain the expense avoided by either local governments or ultimate subsidy recipients.

Credit subsidies represent a third form of government subsidy. By extending loans, lending its credit, and/or assuming interest expense to preferred categories of public or private borrowers, the federal government enables ensuing beneficiaries to obtain funding for projects at either preferred rates of interest or at unusually favorable repayment terms. There are four recognized types of government credit subsidies: (1) the government itself bears either a portion of, or the entire, interest expense; (2) the government acts as the lender at preferred rates; (3) the government guarantees loans enabling a borrower to obtain credit in the private sector which could otherwise be obtained only at higher rates or not at all; and (4) the government loans monies which could not otherwise be obtained at any interest rate or repayment schedule.

Benefit-in-kind subsidies, the fourth type of federal aid, are those which occur where government elects to supply goods and/or services to users below accepted market prices, or below cost where a specific market price cannot be ascertained. Examples of this kind of subsidy are payments to AMTRAK, federal grants-in-aid for airports, operation of the federal airways systems, operating payments to urban transit systems including commuter railroads, and administration of the federal highway programs.

So-called purchase subsidies are another form of federal aid in that they provide a mechanism by which federal government supports certain parts of the private sector through purchase of goods or services at a level above the market price or cost. Historically, this form of subsidy was used to support incipient air transportation through public purchase of air-mail services at prices in excess of reasonable costs, thus utilizing the Post Office Department as a mechanism to foster development of an air transportation network.

Finally, regulatory subsidies are those which reflect the government's support of various regulated industries by exercise of powers over major economic features such as entry, price, and operating scope, and over a host of related and other factors. While the cost of such subsidies could, at a minimum, be estimated as equal to the cost of administering such regulation (and has recently been estimated at much larger magnitudes), it is extremely difficult to quantify the benefits which accrue to the beneficiaries of such programs. In some cases, beneficiaries are thought to be the carriers themselves, as has been alleged in the airline and motor carrier industries. In other instances users (shippers) may benefit, as often cited in the case of railroad regulation. Also, such groups as labor are thought to benefit from federal aid, illustrated by examples in the transit and trucking industries.

Order of magnitude estimates of the first four types of subsidies accruing to transportation have been estimated by Congress for fiscal years 1970 and 1975. As shown in table 4-1, identified transportation subsidies increased from $500 million in 1970 to $2.3 billion in 1975, equating to a 360 percent gain over five years. This compares with a 48 percent increase in total identified federal subsidies to all endeavors during the same period of time. From 1970 to 1975 transportation's share (first four types only) of total federal subsidies increased from less than 1 percent to 2.4 percent. While it is significant to note that transportation subsidies, as identified by Congress, are increasing at a rapid rate, it is also of major importance to understand that the $2.3 billion in 1975 is probably grossly understated if the broadest definition of subsidy is accepted. Not only are several specific direct and indirect subsidies omitted (for example, UMTA alone spent a total of over $1.4 billion in 1975), but also excluded from table 4-1 is regulatory relief, estimated by a noted transportation economist, Dr. Thomas G. Moore, to be between $6.5 billion and $15.2 billion in 1975,[4] in just the surface freight portions of transportation. This so-called economic loss to the public is allegedly due to government control which results in inefficient use of mode, traffic not shifted to alternate modes, and traffic not carried. Regulatory subsidies are highly controversial, and, in fact, the ICC refuted Moore's figures in concluding that regulation provided the public with net benefits vis-à-vis a free market economy.[5] While neither Moore's nor the ICC's figures are rationally supported, the overwhelming consensus of those familiar with transportation

Table 4-1
Nature and Amount of Federal Subsidies Quantified by Joint
Economic Committee, FY 1970 and FY 1975
(millions of dollars)

	Total		Transportation	
Subsidy Form	*1970*	*1975*	*1970*	*1975*
Direct cash	$11.6	$12.3	$0.3	$0.6
Tax	39.9	59.7	–	0.1
Credit	4.1	2.9	–	–
Benefit-in-kind	8.8	20.2	0.2	1.7
Order of magnitude total	$64.4	$95.1	$0.5	$2.3

Source: *Federal Subsidy Programs*, Joint Committee Print, 93rd Congress, 2nd Session, October 18, 1974, p. 5.

Note: Total subsidies include those directed to agriculture, food, health, manpower, education, international, housing, natural resources, transportation, commerce, and other while transportation subsidies include air-carrier payments, construction-differential subsidies (maritime), operating-differential subsidies (maritime), deferral of tax on shipping companies, rail freight-car amortization, airport-development and airport-planning grants, urban mass transit capital-improvement grants, National Railroad Passenger Corporation, and small navigation projects.

regulation is that some public cost is incurred (possibly in exchange for service stability and cross-subsidization of small markets) from economic regulation. Thus the $2.3 billion transportation subsidy estimated by Congress for 1975 is undoubtedly understated, but its comparison to the 1970 figure provides a basis for evaluating the magnitude of increased aid in recent years.

Historic Modal Benefits

Federal funds have aided the construction of, among other facilities, canals, rail trackage, ships, highways, locks, dams, airports, navigation aids, bridges, tunnels, and pipelines. Aside from physical facilities, operating and planning funds have also been designated for the various modes providing freight and passenger service. Presented below are brief discussions of federal aid to five transport recipients: railroads, inland waterways, highways, aviation, and urban transit. Estimates of subsidies are not all-inclusive, nor are they intended to represent precision. Rather, they are ball-park figures exemplifying trends, and represent the state-of-the-art in data availability.

Railroads

The railroad industry has a long tradition of receiving public aid for construction, and more recently the industry has benefited from an infusion of planning money geared to retain and upgrade specified services. The federal government played a significant role in the provision of assets for railroads furing the principal era of their construction between 1850 and 1875. About 7 percent of all land in the continental United States was granted to railroad companies to foster economic development. As shown in table 4-2, 130 million acres were granted to western railroads; states contributed 49 million acres. Aside from the general goal of national economic development, federal land grants to railroads were made for two purposes: they provided railroads with the necessary rights-of-way for construction, and revenues derived by railroads from the sale of excess lands were used to finance construction. Railroads have demonstrated that they repaid the value of land grants several times over (although this point is controversial) in the form of first, free transportation of government property, and later, carriage at reduced rates—commonly referred to as Section 22 rates, identifying the applicable section of the ICC Act. At any rate, the land-grant subsidies were available during a critical stage of railroad development and provided them with an impetus for rapid expansion.

Federal support of railway construction was not limited to grants of land. Federal surveys were undertaken on behalf of railroads although their cost was far less than the value of land grants. In addition, it was determined that the high protective import duties on iron were adversely affecting railroad construc-

Table 4-2
Federal Land Grants to Railroads
(listed by present railroads)

Railroad System	Acreage	Percent of Total
Burlington Northern	39,843,053	31
Southern Pacific	21,648,681	17
Union Pacific	18,979,659	14
Atchison, Topeka & Santa Fe	14,886,795	11
Chicago & North Western	7,302,338	6
Missouri Pacific	3,749,157	3
Seaboard Coast Line	1,843,922	1
All other systems and independently operated railroads	22,050,063	17
Total	130,303,668	100

Source: *Federal Coordinator*, Vol. II, p. 32.

tion, and therefore these duties were remitted to railroads for iron used in railroad construction. The federal government permitted railroads to use natural resources such as timber and stone from public lands adjacent to construction at no cost, and provided construction loans on favorable terms. Finally, in 1864 the Pacific Railroad Act of 1862 was amended to provide federal loans to railroads (bonds) to be repaid in thirty years at a 6 percent interest rate, contingent upon railroad profits. Based on the relatively low interest rate and delayed payments, the railroad industry benefited from such federal support.

Additional federal loans to railroads were provided through the Transportation Act of 1920, the Reconstruction Finance Corporation (established in 1932 and terminated in 1957), the Transportation Act of 1958,[6] the Emergency Rail Services Act of 1970,[7] and the Emergency Rail Restoration Act of 1972.[8] The net effect of such loans weighed against government takeover of the industry during World War I, and alleged disadvantages of economic regulation are open to question. If, in fact, economic regulation had adversely affected railroads, especially in the area of pricing, then it is interesting to note that the federal government spends public funds both to promote and to suppress the railroad industry. In essence, if federal funds are used to reverse adversities caused by federal funds, then national transportation policy needs a massive restructuring in order to conform with overall domestic, economic objectives.

In recent years, three railroad bills were passed which have widened the scope of federal involvement in that industry. The Rail Passenger Service Act of 1970 created the National Railroad Passenger Corporation (AMTRAK), which essentially established intercity rail passenger service as a government operation. In 1973 the Regional Rail Reorganization Act (3-R Act) benefited railroads in a number of ways: (1) the Untied States Railway Association was created to develop a so-called "final system plan" for the railroad industry; (2) Consolidated Rail Corporation (Conrail) was created out of bankrupt northeastern railroads and funds were provided for start-up and operation; (3) states became eligible for funding to maintain local rail services, with up to 5 percent of their allotted monies available for state rail planning; and (4) employees were protected from transactions resulting from federally funded rail planning. Then, in 1976, the Railroad Revitalization and Regulatory Reform Act (4-R Act) was passed: (1) establishing the Rail Services Planning Office (RSPO) as a branch of the ICC to carry out railroad planning; (2) providing funds to subsidize light-density rail lines; (3) creating a cash fund to provide grants for facility maintenance, rehabilitation, improvements, and acquisition, among other endeavors; (4) instituting the Northeast Corridor improvement project which provided ensuing funds to upgrade passenger, freight, and commuter service within and adjacent to the Corridor, and (5) strengthened the 3-R Act provision to maintain and/or provide local rail service.

Railroad planning is currently undertaken by a host of federal agencies including DOT, especially the Federal Railroad Administration, the ICC (RSPO and the Bureau of Economics, among others), and the United States Railway Association (USRA). In fact, RSPO sets the standards to determine cost allocation for railroads providing commuter service under contract to public transit agencies. USRA designated the so-called "final system plan" of railroad service in the East, including commuter lines, and UMTA administers the funding. Furthermore, such federally financed entities as AMTRAK and ConRail also partake in railroad planning. Passenger service is overwhelmingly in the public domain, as is a significant amount of freight service in the Northeast. Most of the fifty states have received rail planning funds from the federal government, and have developed preliminary state plans. With several Midwest railroads on the brink of financial insolvency, the recent accelerated rate of federal involvement in the railroad industry may be more than a short-term phenomenon.

Inland Waterways

Federal expenditures on waterway activities include obligations related to construction, operation, and maintenance of channels and harbors, locks and dams, navigation-related bridge operations as well as engineering and design covering inland waterways, intracoastal waterways, Great Lakes, and coastal harbors. Federal promotion of water carriage was instituted in tariff acts passed during the infancy of our nation. Consequently, in the early 1800s Congress provided funds for many waterway projects, including construction of canals, which not only addressed the goal of promoting commerce, but also responded to defense and navigational (flood control and irrigation) needs. In fact, just as with railroads, throughout the nineteenth century land grants for the purposes of raising capital, constructing canals, and improving rivers were made by the federal government. Such grants have been estimated at about 6.9 million acres— 4.6 million for canal construction and 2.3 million for river improvement.[9] Also, between 1824 and 1828, during the "Era of National Projects," federal funds were provided to purchase canal company stock. Later, in the mid-1800s, Congress fostered the U.S. Merchant Marine through the use of mail subsidies. An additional intent of the mail subsidy was to encourage the use of ships which could be converted as necessary to national defense purposes.

The major impetus of national waterway policy occurred in the early 1900s, when in 1907 and 1909 the Inland Waterways' Commission and the National Waterways' Commission were respectively established. Subsequently, Congress began not only to provide loans for construction, but also to direct payments for promoting the industry. During World War I the U.S. Railroad Administration provided funds for construction, and also directed and carried out the repair and upgrading of several canals and river facilities. After the war, this program was continued, but was transferred to the Inland Waterways Corporation. The coroporation was essentially created in 1924 to last for five years and undertake waterways planning, but lasted until 1953, when it sold its operations to a private company. Over the twenty-nine-year period, the corporation loaned money to state and local governments for construction of waterway terminals, and in turn leased the facilities.

Presently, water carriers benefit from several large government subsidies. Unlike other carriers, inland water carriers pay no user charges—that is, no tolls or taxes on their rights-of-way. Yet, the Army Corps of Engineers is responsible for the construction and maintenance of the inland waterway system. The Corps' duties include flood control, hydropower development, fish and wildlife management, military construction and management, and the overall construction and maintenance of inland waterways. This latter responsibility includes ensuring that waterway depths are sufficient to permit safe operation. A number of other subsidy programs have also been created through legislation for the distinct purpose of aiding the United States Merchant Marine. Specifically, the Merchant Marine Act of 1936 provided for construction differential subsidies, whereby the federal government pays excesses in construction costs over foreign construction costs for vessels manufactured in domestic shipyards. Also, operating differential subsidies are paid to reimburse U.S. ship operators to the extent that their operating costs exceed those of foreign operators. Both construction and operating subsidies are administered by the Federal Maritime Administration, Department of Commerce. This agency is one of the few federal promotional agencies outside the organization and responsibilities of DOT and thus provides an obvious point of controversy. Other aids include: guaranteed construction loans, direct ship construction mortgage assistance, special tax benefits, regulations requiring that one-half of government financed cargoes be carried in American ships, restriction of U.S. coastal trade to U.S. ships, and regulations mandating that U.S. exports purchased through U.S. loans be carried in U.S. ships. Also, lighthouses and marker buoys are installed and maintained by the Coast Guard, and radio fixes are provided to vessels without charge (by contrast with practice in some other nations). Similarly, the National Weather Service provides navigational aids through various forecasting programs. Finally, federal assistance has been supplemented by several coastal states, which have established special-purpose port development authorities to install wharves, docks, warehouses, and loading facilities in their harbors, and to monitor rate relationships in their tributary areas. The lack of waterway user charges has been a traditional transportation issue. Those favoring such charges generally base their arguments on economic grounds—that is, that users (carriers) should pay at least some portion of operating costs as do airlines for airport use, motor carriers for highways, and railroads for rights-of-way and roadbeds. In fact, every president since Franklin D. Roosevelt has recommended a system of water-carrier user charges. Advocates of the status quo argue for tradition, the desire for low-cost water transport, and the need to protect jobs. James J. Kilpatrick, noted contemporary journalist, observes that those against user charges favor more research and study. He aptly states that "under the cynical orthography of politics, the word study is spelled S-t-a-l-l."[10] In essence, while waterway improvements and subsidies by the federal government aid more than just the water-carrier industry, a totally free ride for inland water carriers represents both direct and indirect subsidization.

Highways

Except for colonial toll roads, and a few roads in the post–World War II period, provision of roads and streets has always been a government responsibility. Originally the states, counties, and municipalities bore the burden. After a brief venture at the beginning of the nineteenth century, in the form of the National Pike, the federal government moved into the highway business to stay in 1916. The Pershing Map, drawn at that time, became the national interstate system, constructed after passage of the 1956 Highway Act. Today, highway, road, and street construction and maintenance are financed by a combination of federal, state, and local funds.

The first federally aided road was the National Pike, also known as the Cumberland Road, financed by congressional action in 1906. During the next several decades other so-called national highways were financed by federal grants, and occasionally aided in constuction by the military. A number of roads were financed through the sale of federal land grants, whereby a certain percentage of land proceeds were designated as highway funds. Other land grants were made solely for highway rights-of-way; these latter grants were estimated at about 3.4 million acres through 1934.[11] Little highway construction occurred in the second half of the nineteenth century, mainly because of the Civil War, a shift in emphasis to canal and rail-line construction, and losses incurred by turnpike companies.

Eventually, in 1916, the realization of motor vehicle potential coupled with the industrial revolution prodded Congress to enact the Federal Aid Road Act, which established the current federal-state financing program—a 50 percent sharing of construction costs with state maintenance responsibility. The Federal Highway Act of 1921 limited federal aid to each state up to 7 percent of total existing state mileage. During the 1930s, depression policies resulted in additional federal funds to help states meet their matching shares—in some cases, to construct feeder roads without matching requirements. In fact, beginning in 1936 rural roads became eligible for matching grants. Furthermore, during the 1930s road building was accelerated by the use of previously unemployed persons, as programs to regain countrywide economic health became a federal priority.

The Federal Aid Highway Act of 1944 designed a national interstate system of highways not to exceed 40,000 miles, and to interconnect major economic centers. Federal funds were to be appropriated to states as follows:

Type of Road System	Percent of Federal Funds
Primary	45%
Secondary	30
Urban	25
	100%

Federal criteria were established for fund allocations. In the case of both primary and secondary roads, criteria were the ratios of each state's rural area population, and mileage, to similar data for the country as a whole. For urban roads, the standard is each state's population in communities of 5,000 or more population as a percentage of the similar population measure for the country as a whole. In 1952, the Federal-Aid Highway Act designated specific tax revenues which were to be used for construction of the interstate system.

In 1956 the interstate system received its major boost. The 1956 Federal-Aid Highway Act established a Federal Highway Trust Fund, increased certain existing federal excise taxes, and established additional such taxes. Federal funds allocated to states from the Trust Fund were to be on the basis of 90 percent, with the remaining 10 percent of highway cost funded by state monies. The act also required that so-called ABC funds (funds for primary, secondary, and urban roads) were to be matched on a 50-50 basis and to have first claim on Highway Trust Fund money. The Interstate System of Highways was originally to be completed in 1972, whereas the Highway Trust Fund was to be discontinued. However, several extensions have been made, with the Federal-Aid Highway Act of 1976 setting 1979 as the completion year. Currently, controversy centers on continuation of the fund for purposes of highway, bridge, and tunnel maintenance.

As shown in table 4-3, almost one million miles of our country's highways, roads, and streets have been aided by federal support. It is interesting to note in table 4-3 that the largest beneficiaries (states) of federally aided roads are not the highly populated states of California and New York, but rather Texas (No. 1), Iowa (No. 2), Minnesota (No. 3), Michigan (No. 4), and North Carolina (No. 5). There is little doubt that state benefits from federally aided roads are neither in proportion to population, number of drivers, or revenue contributed to the Highway Trust Fund.

Aviation

The federal government assumed a responsibility to foster commercial aviation in 1926 when air-mail contracts were let to domestic air carriers. Previously, the

Post Office had operated its own air-mail service, including a transcontinental route between New York and San Francisco. Induced by the Kelly Act in 1925, air-mail revenues initially represented a significant portion of air-carrier revenue. Revenues were aided by the Watres Act of 1930, which related government payments to operating costs rather than volume of mail carried. Soon thereafter, other criteria for federal mail payments were adopted, including airplane size, safety equipment, and terrain factors. Then the Airmail Act of 1934 was passed, opening air-mail routes to competitive bidding and placing the program under the authority of the ICC.

Aside from aid to airlines in the early years of aviation, federal assistance was also provided for airway and airport development. The Air Commerce Act of 1926 provided for public (Department of Commerce) operation and maintenance of navigation facilities except airports; airport aid was legislated in 1938. In spite of the 1926 prohibition, in the early 1930s airport construction was aided by federal work-relief projects administered by the Civil Works Administration until 1934. Subsequently, such projects were managed by the Federal Emergency Administration, the Works Program Administration, and the Public Works Administration. Airways extend five miles on both sides of straight lines connecting ground points, and domestic airway facilities have been provided by the federal government since 1926.

The Civil Aeronautics Act of 1938, which established the regulatory framework for commercial air transportation as we now know it, officially provided for subsidy in the form of payments for carrying air mail. The act required that mail pay rates be set at levels to produce mail revenues which, together with revenues from all other sources (that is, passenger and goods) would permit well-managed carriers to survive and grow. In other words, operating deficits were covered by mail pay in whatever amount necessary. The act also authorized the board to evaluate the airport system in order to determine the desirable extent of federal participation in airport planning, construction, operation, and maintenance. Recommendations of government involvement were made in 1939 but were preempted by World War II. Yet the recommendations were the impetus for the passage of the Federal Airport Act of 1946, which not only provided a program of aid for airport development but required the formulation of an annual National Airport Plan to meet the needs of civil aviation.

In 1953 airline subsidies were distinctly separated from air-mail compensation. The Post Office then began paying (and still does) air-mail compensation based on CAB determinations, and the board was to make airline subsidy payments. The Federal Aviation Act of 1958 created the Federal Aviation Agency essentially to carry out the provisions of the similar 1946 act. This agency is now a component of DOT. Postal, airway, and airport subsidization continued in a rather stable fashion until 1970, when the Airport and Airway Improvement Act was passed, extending all aviation aid, but changing the method of financing. Similar to the highway situation, an Aviation Trust Fund was established col-

Table 4–3
Federally Aided Highway Mileage by State

State	Primary System	Other	Total
Alabama	10,466	11,624	22,090
Alaska	4,165	—	4,165
Arizona	5,199	2,822	8,021
Arkansas	14,610	4,378	18,988
California	14,320	13,543	27,863
Colorado	9,016	1,071	10,087
Connecticut	1,075	1,909	2,984
Delaware	631	1,480	2,111
Dist. of Col.	—	264	264
Florida	11,535	8,655	20,190
Georgia	17,659	11,266	28,925
Hawaii	493	525	1,018
Idaho	4,981	3,974	8,955
Illinois	14,536	13,265	27,801
Indiana	11,071	14,195	25,266
Iowa	9,839	33,387	43,226
Kansas	10,419	21,910	32,329
Kentucky	3,988	15,496	19,484
Louisiana	4,770	8,112	12,882
Maine	3,711	901	4,612
Maryland	1,088	8,728	9,816
Massachusetts	2,640	3,769	6,409
Michigan	9,274	26,995	36,269
Minnesota	12,145	26,721	38,866
Mississippi	10,621	12,772	23,393
Missouri	7,781	24,866	32,647
Montana	6,359	6,206	12,565
Nebraska	9,861	13,810	23,671
Nevada	2,248	3,922	6,170
New Hampshire	1,827	1,319	3,146
New Jersey	2,057	3,052	5,109
New Mexico	10,137	518	10,655
New York	15,901	13,602	29,503
North Carolina	13,330	20,460	33,790
North Dakota	6,974	11,981	18,955
Ohio	18,421	11,607	30,028
Oklahoma	12,008	11,326	23,334
Oregon	4,837	8,462	13,299
Pennsylvania	14,416	7,942	22,358
Rhode Island	868	263	1,131
South Carolina	9,748	17,059	26,807
South Dakota	8,431	11,365	19,796
Tennessee	9,671	9,126	18,797
Texas	59,241	739	59,980
Utah	5,125	1,934	7,059

State	Primary System	Other	Total
Vermont	2,601	891	3,492
Virginia	9,432	15,497	24,929
Washington	6,850	9,628	16,478
West Virginia	5,348	8,213	13,561
Wisconsin	11,920	15,438	27,358
Wyoming	6,079	563	6,642
Total	449,723	477,551	927,274

Source: Federal Highway Administration, Department of Transportation.

lecting revenues from six sources: (1) tax on air freight, (2) flat dollar tax per overseas customer, (3) annual aircraft registration fee, (4) per-pound registration fee on jet aircraft, (5) per-pound registration fee on poston aircraft, and (6) fuel tax on noncommercial flights. The passenger excise tax provides the largest revenue source to the Trust Fund. Grants are made to local governments on a 50-50 matching basis, and are to be used for the operational aspects of airports.

Finally, the aviation industry is subsidized by federally granted loans of up to 40 percent, for the purchase of equipment by local, short-haul, and feeder air carriers. The loan program was begun in 1957 and is administered by the Federal Aviation Administration. From 1967 through 1977, thirty-seven such loans were provided for the purchase of about $248 million of equipment; loans totaled $216 million, equating to 87 percent of expended funds.[12]

Urban Transit

Transportation in urban areas quite naturally benefits from federal aid to highways, but other more direct benefits have been provided by assistance from the Urban Mass Transportation Administration (UMTA), DOT. Instituted by the Urban Mass Transportation Act of 1964, UMTA provides funds for planning, operating, and constructing transit systems, including the purchase of equipment. So-called capital grants of up to 80 percent of net project cost are provided for the purchase of facilities and equipment; other grants fo 100 percent are made for technical assistance (planning). Also, loans are available to finance the acquisition and leasing of property for use as rights-of-way and stations.

The Urban Mass Transportation Assistance Act of 1970 not only provided planning funds but also directed UMTA to study the desirability of helping mass transportation companies in urban areas defray operating losses. As a result of ensuing study, federal grants became available on a 50-50 matching basis to subsidize operating deficits. Then, in 1974 the Urban Mass Transportation Assistance Act provided grants of up to 80 percent of cost, for studying the expected impact of instituting fare-free mass transportation. A number of cities were chosen for development of demonstration projects.

Currently, UMTA funds extend to a wide variety of urban transit endeavors, reaching 442 of the nation's transit properties.[13] The completed rapid-rail system in San Francisco (BART) was federally aided, as are the systems currently being constructed in the cities of Atlanta, Baltimore, Honolulu, and Washington. Operating subsidies are made to bus systems throughout the nation and one UMTA-funded demonstration people mover operates in Morgantown, West Virginia. Other people movers are planned or under study in eleven other cities. Planning assistance is ubiquitous.

Scope and Growth of Subsidies

It has already been demonstrated that federal aid to transportation is broad-scoped, widening in coverage, and growing in magnitude. This section not only affirms these conclusions by providing quantitative evidence, but shows that previous estimates understate the real level of federal subsidy. While an accurate accounting of federal subsidies to transportation is at best controversial, an order of magnitude can be inferred by adding, to a previously calculated figure, certain estimates for excluded subsidies.

Table 4-1 estimated that in 1975 transportation subsidies amounted to $2.3 billion, yet this figure excludes regulatory subsidies and several other indirect federal aids which are commonly omitted from subsidy discussions. Regulatory subsidies are too hypothetical and lacking in supportive evidence to be estimated for purposes of this book, but speculation is that even if prior estimates of $10 billion are high (see Chapter 2), the figure is probably at least in the billions. Other transportation subsidies excluded from table 4-1 are discussed below.

1. AMTRAK enjoys federal loan guarantees, as presented in table 4-4. These loans are somewhat of a credit subsidy in that AMTRAK is able either to obtain money at favorable interest rates or obtain capital it might not have been able otherwise to attract. AMTRAK's ability to finance long-term capital programs at short-term rates was recognized by the ICC in 1975 when it found:

    By using the short-term financing route, Amtrak has attempted to take advantage of the lower interest rates usually available on short-term debt compared to long-term debt. The carrier is able to obtain short-term financing, because the Federal guarantee feature virtually assures an ability to roll over the notes at maturity. The preponderance of short-term financing probably worked against the company in 1974 because short-term interest rates were higher than long-term rates, but it may have prevented Amtrak from being locked into a long range commitment at near-record high interest rates in 1974.[14]

Table 4–4
Federal Loan Guarantees for Amtrak 1971–1975
(hundred thousand dollars)

Year	Obtained	Repaid	Outstanding
1971	$ 30.0	$ 5.0	$ 25.0
1972	65.0	90.0	—
1973	144.5	25.0	119.5
1974	581.3	407.1	293.7
1975	993.2	785.7	501.2[a]

Source: Interstate Commerce Commission, *Report to the President and the Congress, Effectiveness of the Act, March 15, 1976, AMTRAK*, Appendix 8.
[a]Includes $123.5 million committed for, less purchase agreement.

AMTRAK's unique relationship to the federal government makes it difficult to assess the value of these loan guarantees. To the extent that the federal government is avoiding expense through AMTRAK loan guarantees, it is in effect reducing its subsidy cost. Thus, unless AMTRAK becomes profitable, loan guarantees are a form of subsidy, but not to the extent of the differentiation between AMTRAK and market interest rates.

2. Two indirect types of airline subsidies are investment tax credits and maintenance of the CAB. In 1975, CAB expenses and salaries totaled $18 million.[15] This kind of administrative study was excluded from the surface-freight regulatory subsidy estimated at about $10 billion by Moore. Although it is difficult to quantify benefits which flow to recipients of this subsidy, it is nonetheless recognized as such since the CAB protects the intercity air passenger industry by: (1) administering subsidy payments, (2) restricting competition, and (3) allowing cross-subsidy of services through its control over fares. The second form of indirect federal support to airlines, shown in table 4–5, is the investment tax credit. For the years 1971 through 1975 airline use of the investment tax credit ranged from $27 million to $45 million. The CAB does not summarize these data; they are available only from individual carrier reports.

3. Air carriers have occasionally received credit subsidies from federal loan guarantees. Table 4–6 displays loans obtained by airlines, and their federally guaranteed portions, from 1958 to 1974. The value of these loan guarantees is both difficult to determine and relatively minor when measured against other subsidies received by air carriers.

4. Although federally aided highways are constructed on a pay-as-you-go basis, as seen in table 4–7 from 1956 through 1975 a shortfall (expenditures minus payments) of $28.7 billion was generated. Furthermore, with one minor exception in 1973, this deficit has been increasing annually for every

Table 4-5
Indirect Federal Aid to Airlines, 1971-1975
(millions of dollars)

Year	Investment Tax Credits	CAB	Total
1971	$45	$12	$57
1972	30	14	44
1973	27	14	41
1974	26	16	42
1975	35	18	53

Source: Civil Aeronautics Board, *Annual Reports, Form 41.* Subcommittee on the Committee on Appropriations, House of Representatives, *Hearings on Department of Transportation and Related Agencies Appropriations for 1977, 94th Congress, 2nd Session, Part 4.*
Note: Investment tax credit data was calculated for the years 1971 through 1975 only.

year since 1969. Consequently, a recent study by the Urban Institute concluded that "data for the past two decades indicated that for the road system as a whole, Congressional concern for equity was not met. Road users did not pay enough to cover the expenditures made on their behalf."[16]

5. A major focus of interest surrounding highway financing is the determination of what would be a fair share of each classification of user. In a 1969 study by the Federal Highway Administration (DOT), automobiles were found to be the largest supported of the Highway Trust Fund as shown below.[17] This study concluded that intercity buses had a cost responsibility

Classification of Vehicle		Percentage Distribution to Highway Trust Fund
Automobile		60.36%
Trucks		38.06
single unit	(22.59%)	
combination	(15.47)	
Buses		1.30
transit	(0.45)	
intercity	(0.39)	
school	(0.46)	
Publicly Owned		0.28
TOTAL		100.00%

for .43 percent of the Highway Trust Fund, but paid only .39 percent. Although the Urban Institute study (note 16) concluded nothing about buses in particular, it did state that "light vehicle payments exceeded their costs by an enormous margin for both pay-as-you-go and road-as-industry approaches."[18] If either of the two above studies is correct, then highway underpayments are caused by trucks, buses, or both.

Table 4-6
Federal Loan Guarantees for Airline Flight Equipment, 1958-1974
(hundred thousand dollars)

Year	Total Loan	Guaranteed Portion
1958	$14.7	$13.2
1959	10.3	9.3
1960	3.8	3.4
1961	8.0	7.2
1962	5.1	4.6
1963	.9	.8
1964	6.5	5.8
1965	.4	.4
1966	2.8	2.5
1967	2.7	2.4
1968	—	—
1969	—	—
1970	—	—
1971	—	—
1972	—	—
1973	27.0	24.3
1974	10.6	9.6

Source: Civil Aeronautics Board, *Handbook of Airline Statistics*, 1973 and 1975 Supplement.

6. Because of the magnitude of expenditures, highways are financed with bonds issued by government agencies—usually states. Historically, these bonds have lower interest rates than commercial bonds because of the tax-free provisions affecting interest payments, and, in many cases, the full faith and credit provisions of government agencies supported by the power to tax. Thus, incrementally reduced interest payments (corporate rates minus municipal rates times the principal outstanding) represent benefits to highway users in that they pay less to support the roads than if such bonds did not enjoy tax-free provisions. Likewise, taxes related to highway use are also lower because of government control, since these taxes pay lower-than-market interest rates; also highway authorities are exempt from paying certain taxes that would be incurred by private funding agencies, not to mention "ad valorem" property taxes.

The magnitude of government support relating to tax-free bonds can be demonstrated by comparing municipal and state with corporate bond interest rates for similarly rated bonds. For instance, table 4-8 shows that $840 million of highway-related municipal bonds were issued in 1966. Assuming that the average interest rate of these bonds was 2 percent below that of comparably

Table 4–7
Comparison of Total Expenditures and Total Payments for Highways
1956–1975
(hundred thousand dollars)

Year	Total Expenditures	Total Payments	Shortfall
1956	$ 7,123	$ 7,520	$ (397)
1957	8,014	8,304	(290)
1958	9,380	8,124	1,256
1959	10,178	9,153	1,025
1960	10,073	9,496	577
1961	10,726	10,143	583
1962	11,311	11,022	289
1963	11,961	11,797	164
1964	12,780	12,647	133
1965	13,401	13,270	131
1966	14,738	13,543	1,195
1967	15,489	14,099	1,390
1968	16,711	15,439	1,272
1969	17,529	17,055	474
1970	19,800	17,679	2,121
1971	21,407	18,841	2,566
1972	22,052	18,210	3,842
1973	22,929	19,827	3,102
1974	24,211	19,968	4,243
1975	26,176	21,194	4,982
Total	$305,989	$277,331	$28,658

Source: Urban Institute, *An Analysis of Road Expenditures and Payments by Vehicle Class (1956–1975)*, February 1977, Tables 1.14 and 1.30.

rated corporate bonds, an annual highway subsidy of about $17 million would have resulted (.02 multiplied by $840 million) in that year. Assuming an average bond maturity date of twenty years (conservative by highway standards), a total interest savings of $340 million would be realized over the life of the bonds.

More recently, highway funding subsidization would naturally be less than in 1966 because of the relative completeness of the Interstate System. Table 4–9 shows that about $670 million of indirect subsidies accrued to highways from lower municipal bond rates from 1972 through 1975. This amount was estimated by: (1) determining average interest rates for corporate and municipal bonds by Moody's bond rating, (2) multiplying the interest-rate differential (1.5 percent to 3.4 percent, depending on the bond) between the two types of bonds times the face value of municipal bonds in order to estimate annual interest subsidization, (3) calculating the average number of years until maturity for municipal bonds,[19] and (4) multiplying the average number of maturity years times annual interest subsidies. Averaging the $670 million over four years

Table 4–8
Municipal Bonds to Support Highway Construction, 1966

Authority	Moody's Rating	Amount ($000)
Georgia Road	AAA	$ 10,000
Georgia Highway	AAA	16,600
Alabama Highway Finance	AA	25,000
Louisiana Highway	AA	30,000
Louisiana Highway	AA	15,000
Louisiana Highway	AA	15,000
Maryland County Highway	AA	2,840
Maryland State Roads	AA	10,000
Maryland State Roads	AA	20,000
New Jersey Turnpike	AA	179,000
Pennsylvania Turnpike	AA	77,500
Pennsylvania Turnpike	AA	77,500
Illinois State Toll	A	14,250
Kentucky Turnpike	A	120,000
Kentucky Turnpike	A	17,500
Florida Development Commission	BAA	23,500
Oklahoma Turnpike Authority	BAA	150,000
Oklahoma Turnpike Authority	BAA	36,000
Total		$839,690

Source: *Moody's Municipal and Government Manual*, Volumes I and II, 1976.

equates to $168 million annually, but this is undoubtedly an underestimation of the annual subsidization since the beginning of the Trust Fund in 1956, because of higher-valued municipal issues prior to 1972. For instance, as table 4-8 showed, 1966 highway-related municipal bonds had a face value of $840 million; this compares with $150 million in 1975 and $137 million in 1974 (table 4-9).

In order to estimate the interest subsidy accruing to highways since 1956, or at least to calculate a more accurate annual average, the total value of highway-related municipal bonds issued from 1956-1975 was determined, and a subsidy ratio developed from table 4-9 was applied to this figure. That table shows a $670 million subsidy for 1972-1975, which is about 47 percent of the $1.4 billion total face value of highway-related municipal bonds issued during that period. Applying this percentage to the $8.0 billion of highway-related municipal bonds issued between 1956 and 1975 results in a twenty-year indirect subsidy of $3.8 billion, and an average annual indirect subsidy of about $190 million.

In summary, the purpose of identifying some of the exceptions to the previously calculated annual transportation subsidy of $2.3 billion was to support the contention that the figure is grossly understated. This task was

Table 4-9
Estimated Tax Subsidy Value of Municipal Bond Issues, 1972-1975

Bond Rating	Corporate Bonds[a]	Highway Related Municipal Bonds[b]	Differential	Total Value Highway Related Municipal Bonds ($000)	Annual Subsidy[c] ($000)	Average Maturity in Years[b]	Total Subsidy[d] ($000)
			1975				
AAA/A-1	8.785%	5.375%	3.410%	$ 6,000	$ 204.6	6	$ 1,227.6
AA	9.110	7.118	1.992	110,000	2,191.2	11.45	25,089.2
A	9.610	7.500	2.110	34,000	717.4	18	12,913.2
BAA	10.630	—	—	—		—	—
Annual Subsidy				$ 150,000			$ 39,230.0
			1974				
AAA/A-1	8.565	5.425	3.140	20,545	645.1	6	3,870.6
AA	8.705	6.979	1.726	89,150	1,538.7	8.25	12,694.3
A	9.140	7.250	1.890	27,270	515.4	16	8,246.4
BAA	9.580	—	—	—		—	—
Annual Subsidy				$ 136,965			$ 24,811.3
			1973				
AAA/A-1	7.435	5.332	2.103	209,500	4,405.8	28.95	127,547.9
AA	7.645	5.500	2.145	97,150	2,083.9	8.26	17,213.0
A	7.855	5.718	2.137	216,500	4,626.6	29.51	136,531.0
BAA	8.280	6.399	1.881	80,000	1,504.8	12.00	18,057.6
Annual Subsidy				$ 603,150			$299,349.5

1972

AAA/A-1	7.210	4.740	2.470	124,000	3,062.8	27.90	85,452.1
AA	7.490	5.522	1.968	200,685	3,949.5	30.01	118,524.5
A	7.650	6.166	1.484	208,400	3,092.7	33.24	102,801.3
BAA	8.090	—	—	—	—	—	—
Annual Subsidy				$ 533,085			$306,777.9
Grand Total 1972–1975				$1,423,200			$670,168.7

Source: *Moody's Corporate Manual* and *Moody's Municipal and Government Manual*, 1972–1975.

[a] Average of average high and low.

[b] Weighted average.

[c] Interest rate differential times amount of Municipal Bonds issued.

[d] Annual subsidy times average maturity in years.

accomplished even though some indirect subsidies have undoubtedly been excluded from the discussion. However, none of the excluded subsidies is likely to approach regulatory benefits which, if properly calculated, may inflate the $2.3 billion by several-fold. In essence, transportation subsidies are not what they appear to be—they are much greater.

Regulatory Trends

The regulatory framework of interstate commerce has remained virtually unchanged since the passage of the Interstate Commerce Act of 1887, as amended, and the Civil Aeronautics Act of 1938. While regulatory criteria have shifted in some areas, as have responsibilities of various public agencies overseeing regulation, interstate carriers are still subject to public control over entry, rates, routes, mergers, acquisitions, and abandonments of service. Regulation and its multitude of components have been much discussed and analyzed in the research studies identified in Chapter 2, and in Appendixes A-1 through A-12. Emphasis on regulatory matters is natural because federal regulation of economic factors is foreign to normal market interplay. Thus, once control such as price regulation is enacted, questions arise in geometric fashion. What criterion should be used to control maximum versus minimum rates? How should prices relate to cost? Is long-run marginal or short-run fully allocated cost applicable as a rate-making standard? How should the cost of capital be measured? Are "fair" earnings a function of capital structure, financial leveraging, and/or management efficiency? What is the relationship among reasonable rates and entry, dividend policy, risk, productivity, and operating authority?

This book does not attempt to identify the details of regulatory policy for several reasons. First, such policies have been more than adequately covered in the literature as exemplified by the many references provided in previous chapters. Second, regulatory policies are largely revealed by thousands of ICC, CAB, and FMC annual decisions (the ICC acts on 5,000-6,000 annual applications for motor common carrier operating certificates) and the magnitude and broad scope of the decisions make it virtually impossible to evaluate regulation comprehensively. Third, and finally, many regulatory decisions are made on an "ad hoc" basis with no consistent thread of philosophy or criterion. As one example, ICC criteria for determining revenue need of truck operators have switched from a sole reliance on a 93 percent operating ratio to a standard of return on equity (net profit over stockholders' equity), to return on investment (operating income over book value of net depreciated investment in operating property), to a vague combination of factors including all of the above measures in addition to capitalization ratios, cash flow, and other financial indicators.[20] In the case of railroads, regulatory criteria to determine reasonable rates have traditionally been enigmatic. In essence, regulatory criteria are so elusive that for purposes of this book, a recognition of this character, along with subsequent comments, will suffice.

What is of significance herein are two general trends evident across regulatory policies, and the implications of such trends relative to the federal role in transportation. These somewhat contradictory trends are a movement toward deregulation in either part (regulatory reform) or whole, and a tendency to promote transportation within a regulatory framework. As discussed below, research studies may have played some role in influencing the direction and magnitude of these trends; contrarily, research at least appears to have given little attention to the contradictions of recent federal regulatory movements.

In the past decade, much discussion has centered on the prospects of economic deregulation, and what was essentially a bill to deregulate many areas of the interstate trucking industry was sponsored by DOT in 1976.[21] Likewise, similar legislation for the airline industry (Cannon-Kennedy Bill S. 689 and Pearson-Baker Bill S. 292) was the topic of congressional hearings in 1977. However, no such legislation has been forthcoming, and the emphasis appears to have shifted from deregulation to reform (that is, a milder form of, or partial, deregulation). In fact, one year after supporting deregulation, DOT revolved to a position of defending regulation. In his first speech as Secretary of Transportation, Brock Adams stated that

... deregulation ... has been sold on the theory that it would protect the consumer by allowing market forces to work more effectively, and, in theory, lower prices and better services would result.

I have not accepted this theory ... because the whole history of American transportation has been one of having to regulate industry with monopolistic tendencies. This regulation was designed to prevent powerful economic forces from controlling transportation, using it to obtain competitive advantages, or from dominating a transportation mode in order to force smaller competitors out of business.[22]

Suggestions and actual programs of regulatory reform have derived from a number of sources. The Senate Committee on Government Operations published a four-volume report on regulation[23] offering a number of suggestions to reform the organizational structure of regulatory agencies. The 4-R Act (1976) liberalized railroad rate-making by stating that a rate cannot be judged to be unreasonably high unless the commission finds that the proposing carrier has "market dominance" over the subject service. Market dominance will be presumed where any one of three conditions exist: (1) where the proponent carrier or carriers have a market share greater than or equal to 70 percent of the relevant market, (2) where the proposed rate equals or exceeds 160 percent of variable costs, or (3) where shippers or consignees have made a substantial investment in rail-related equipment or facilities which prevents or makes impractical the use of another carrier or mode. Also, in 1977 the ICC recommended thirty-nine changes addressing motor-carrier entry regulation.[24] Six changes focused on application proceedings; fourteen dealt with facilitating entry; twelve addressed internal commission operations; four fell within a miscellaneous category; and three related to further study and analysis. Finally, the CAB has become more flexible in allowing airlines pricing freedom and, to a lesser extent, freedom of entry. Examples of a more liberalized entry policy are two former commuter airlines that were recently certificated—Air New England, on January 24, 1975, and Air Midwest, on November 14, 1976. Two devices often proposed as measures of regulatory reform are: (1) a "zone of reasonableness" whereby carriers can raise or lower prices without public interference, and (2) shifting the burden of proof from proponent to protestant in entry cases.

At first glance, regulatory reform appears to mean less federal control of transportation, and thus a contradiction to the increasing public involvement in promoting transportation—that is, unless regulatory reform is a device to aid interstate carriers—a distinct possibility in the case of railroads, but hardly likely for airlines, and certainly remote for motor carriers. On the other hand, regulatory reform, if enacted, could have little impact on government control. First, regulatory commissions will still have control over carrier economic activities, and the administration of regulatory legislation is open to interpretation. Second, reform measures may not be significant. Open-entry policies may have no impact on railroads, little impact on airlines, and, at best, moderate impact on long-haul, less-than-truckload, trucking. In essence, the greatest impact could likely be in short-haul markets, and in some cases, loss of alleged cross-subsidized, short-haul markets would be a blessing to certain airlines and motor carriers. Increased rate freedom may also be somewhat of a theoretical exercise. It has already been reported that railroads are not taking advantage of their newly acquired rate freedom by the 4-R Act,[25] and motor carriers already have significant rate freedom as individual carriers have the right to independent action in opposing rate bureau agreements. Airlines may be most affected by rate freedom in the short run, but in an oligopolistic market such as much of the airline industry, prices have a way of equalizing in the long run (that is, the kinked demand curve), and competition flourishes on the basis of service. Finally, this country has traditionally protected its transportation modes, and if less control of such carriers adversely affects various industries the pendulum would likely swing back to increased regulation and protectionism.

The other major trend of regulatory policies is the provision of promotional devices within a regulatory context. This has been the case for years in regard to labor. For instance, in rate proceedings the increased costs of labor are virtually passed on to consumers without question. Carriers justify higher rates based on increased costs so that a marginal technique is used, and often approved by regulatory agencies, to acquire additional revenue. Labor is also protected in merger proceedings whereby the impact on labor is a major criterion determining regulatory approval or denial of the application. Also, it has long been evident that regulators have avoided the issue of labor power in transportation by virtually eliminating investigation of labor practices from its scope of research and policymaking activities. Finally, an example of labor protection is found in a recent promotional law containing regulatory implications. For years, railroads complained that their common-carrier status restricted them from shedding unprofitable passenger business. On the other hand, urban communities protested against proposed service abandonment on the premise that rail service provided environmental benefits such as less traffic, congestion, noise, pollution, and energy use. Aside from the creation of AMTRAK, the Urban Mass Transportation Act of 1964 was amended to provide for public takeover of railroad commuter service; federal subsidies for public conversion were legislated along with operating subsidies beginning at 100 percent and decreasing over five years to 50 percent (Section 17 of the act). At the same time, as seen in Appendix C, Section 13(c) of the act protected labor "against a worsening of their positions." In essence, by restricting prerogatives of public transit agencies to rid themselves of inefficient rail labor, the federal government simply transferred a railroad problem to local political jurisdictions. Furthermore, Section 13(c) is contrary to the UMT Act's objective of funding socially desirable transit where efforts are made to insure reasonable levels of efficiency.

Aside from labor protection (or promotion), the public lines of regulation and promotion are drawing closer. Safety regulation was transferred from the ICC to DOT during the formation of the latter so that DOT both promotes and regulates transportation. More striking is the recent creation of the Rail Services Planning Office of the ICC, which promotes railroad transportation through its research programs and recommendations of rail policy—especially in regard to mergers. Thus, the ICC also promotes and regulates transportation. As identified in Chapter 2, several recent studies by the CAB advocated a liberalization of economic restrictions; to the degree such policies are carried out by the board, regulatory policies may be changed in the direction of increased industry promotion. Regulatory agencies have always had the ability to promote transportation through their interpretation of legislation and exercise of regulatory criteria, but it has only been in recent years where medium and long-range planning have become functional resonsibilities of such organizations.

Both trends—regulatory liberalization and increased promotion—are rooted in historic transportation research. The BIR, Doyle, and Magnuson reports, among others, all identified regulatory inequities and recommended changes which would liberalize public policy toward various rate, entry, and related restrictions—especially for railroads. Such conclusions do not require data collection, array, and analysis. Rather, they can be reached on the basis of logic and sound economic principles. With an almost-completed interstate highway system and the maturing of alternative means of movement, transportation monopolies and the potential for such are gradually diminishing. Since the ideals of competition are consistent with this country's basic economic system and Puritan ethics, arguments for deregulation are often supported by shallow quantified evidence, but strong economic rationale. Thus, research can address (and has addressed) regulatory restrictions without delving into difficult impact analysis, and at the same time avoiding the ubiquitous problems of parochialism and cost-benefit measurement difficulties. Similarly, almost all major research efforts advocate increased federal involvement in various areas of transportation, either because more research and/or data are required, carriers do not possess the ability to solve their problems, or a body broader than state government is required to address the issues of interstate movement. Furthermore, there appears to be a general attitude among many politicians (the regional problem again) that it is far better (possibly for their sake) to raise federal, rather than state or local, taxes. As discussed in the following chapter the more comprehensive transportation research is initiated and financed by the federal government, and subsequent approaches tend to identify and view issues from a perspective of national problem-solving.

In conclusion, liberalization of regulatory restrictions appears to be somewhat inconsistent with the trend toward increased federal involvement and subsidization of transportation. In the former case certain carriers may be adversely affected, while in the latter instance they may benefit. Yet in the long run the impact on the marketplace may be similar. From strictly a pessimistic perspective both trends could lead in the long run to a reduction in the number of carriers, coupled with increased federal aid.

While projections of events resulting from the above trends are purely speculative, one point is fairly clear. The transportation research environment has traditionally not been conducive to awakening, warning, and influencing public decision-makers to properly address the root causes of transportation policy deficiencies.

Notes

1. As contrasted with, for example, the stimulation received from technological spin-off.

2. *The Economics of Federal Subsidy Programs*, Joint Economic Committee, 92nd Congress, 1st Session, Committee Print, January 11, 1972.

3. *Federal Subsidy Programs*, Joint Committee Print, 93rd Congress, 2nd Session, October 18, 1974, p. 9.

4. Thomas G. Moore, "Deregulating Surface Freight Transportation," *Promoting Competition in Regulated Markets*, The Brookings Institution, 1975.

5. *A Cost and Benefit Evaluation of Surface Transportation Regulation*, Interstate Commerce Commission, January 1976.

6. Loans were provided to seven eastern railroads which eventually went into bankruptcy: Boston and Maine, Central of New Jersey, Erie Lackawanna, Lehigh Valley, New Haven (also New Haven Trustrees), Penn Central, and Reading.

7. Under this act, only the Penn Central and Central Railroad of New Jersey obtained loans.

8. Federally guaranteed loans were received by the Penn Central, Erie Lackawanna, Lehigh Valley, and the Reading.

9. *Transportation: Information Concerning Land Grants for Roads, Canals, River Improvements and Railroads*, U.S. Department of the Interior, 1940, p. 4.

10. James J. Kilpatrick, *Mobile Press-Register*, June 16, 1977.

11. Federal Coordinator of Transportation, Vol. II, p. 8.

12. Data furnished by the Federal Aviation Administration, Department of Transportation and published in *Federal Aid to Domestic Transportation*, Congressional Research Service, Library of Congress, May 16, 1977, p. 107.

13. *Mass Transit* (monthly periodical), June 1977, p. 8.

14. Interstate Commerce Commission, *Report to the President and Congress, Effectiveness of the Act, March 15, 1975 Amtrak*, Volume 1, p. 35.

15. Civil Aeronautics Board functions relate to international and overseas, as well as to domestic air transport, but there is no available apportionment between these diverse jurisdictional areas.

16. Urban Institute, *An Analysis of Road Expenditures and Payments by Vehicle Class* (1956-1975), Washington, D.C., February 1977.

17. *Allocation of Highway Cost Responsibility and Tax Payment, 1969*, Federal Highway Administration, Department of Transportation, May 1970, Table 25.

18. Urban Institute, *An Analysis of Road Expenditures . . .*, p. 49.

19. Where bonds matured serially, the number of years to maturity was divided by two in order to derive average maturity time.

20. Harvey A. Levine, "A Historic Analysis of the Criteria to Determine the Revenue Need of Motor Common Carriers," *ICC Practitioners' Journal*, January-February 1973.

21. *Motor Carrier Reform Act*, U.S. Department of Transportation, December 1976.

22. Speech by Secretary of Transportation Brock Adams to Consumer Federation's Assembly, Washington, D.C., February 10, 1977.

23. *Study on Federal Regulation, Volume I, The Regulatory Appointment Process, January 1977; Volume II, Congressional Oversight of Regulatory Agencies, February 1977; Volume II, Public Participation in Regulatory Agency Proceedings, July 1977; and Volume IV, Delay in the Regulatory Process, July 1977*; Committee on Government Operations, United States Senate, 95th Congress, 1st Session.

24. *Improving Motor-Carrier Entry Regulation*, Report and Recommendations of a Staff Task Force, Interstate Commerce Commission, July 6, 1977.

25. *The Impact of the 4-R Act, Railroad Ratemaking Provisions*, A Report to Congress as Directed by Section 202 of the Railroad Revitalization and Regulatory Reform Act of 1976, Interstate Commerce Commission, October 5, 1977.

5   Research/Policy Connection

Research of overall national transportation policy, and component issues, has far different parameters than does research associated with technology. In the latter instance, the goal is usually linked to "building a better mousetrap," manifested in faster, better-designed, safer, smaller, larger, more productive, more powerful, and/or more efficient machinery. Transportation technology has been advanced where diesel locomotives replaced steam engines, jet aircraft replaced propeller airplanes, and where subway systems replaced buses. Many more examples are not only available for all modes of transport, but also for transportation facilities such as container ports, automated air-cargo facilities, and integrated rail-truck (piggyback) terminals. However, since national transportation policy is somewhat vague, and interpretation of transportation goals is largely a function of the political process, the value of policy research is correspondingly dubious. This is precisely why much transportation research addressing policy has been criticized as aimless, lacking in supporting data, and hypothetical at best. Yet, this is not to say that research has not affected national transportation policy. On the contrary, analysis of those studies identified in Chapter 2 reveals that much research has become an extension of government intervention, and has taken on a self-serving characteristic helping to create and protect the organizational structure and financial means necessary to exercise government control.

This chapter explores the relationship between transportation policy research and the trend toward increasing government involvement by first comparing six major research studies in regard to derivation of issues, identification of issues, and recommendations. Then two case studies are presented which demonstrate: (1) that market interrelationships cause initial public intervention to lead to expanded government control, and (2) once involved, government tends to protect the status quo, even if initial rationale for intervention no longer prevails. Finally, contemporary research is examined to determine if historic trends are being continued, or if signs of change are evident.

Research Policy Relationships

This section examines common features of policy research which not only have historically stimulated increased public involvement and control of transportation, but continue to assume that the federal government is the panacea for nearly all transport deficiencies. Six major research efforts, between 1942 and

1961, were selected for comparative analysis. The rationale for selecting the 1942 Planning Board study as the embarkation point is that it was the initial broad study subsequent to all major modes being regulated, and after the declaration of the formal statement of national transportation policy. The Doyle Report of 1961 represents the latest date of the six sample studies because it was the last major research study prior to the establishment of DOT. Together with the Planning Board and Doyle studies, four other efforts (BIR-1944, Dearing-Owens-1949, Sawyer-1960, and Mueller-1961) comprise the sample compared for derivation of issues, issue identificaiton, and recommendations.

Table 5-1 presents a comparision of the derivation of issues among the six major studies. In all cases but the Mueller Report, a congressional or presidential mandate to analyze public aid and/or national policy set the stage for ensuing study. While the Mueller Report did not technically follow a mandate, it was in response to President Kennedy's budget message and thus in a sense had executive-branch prodding. Similarly, the Planning Board study of 1942 was in response to President Roosevelt's charge; the 1944 BIR study emanated from the Transportation Act of 1940, which required a national investigation of the then-new Policy Statement; the Dearing-Owens study in 1949 was actually part of the Hoover Commission Report authorized by federal legislation; the Sawyer

Table 5-1
Comparison of Issue Derivation among Six Major Transportation Studies, 1942–1961

	Year/Study					
Issue Derivation	*1942 Planning Board*	*1944 BIR*	*1949 D-O*	*1949 Sawyer*	*1960 Mueller*	*1961 Doyle*
Congressional or presidential mandate to analyze public aid and/or national policy	X	X	X	X		X
Current problems as perceived by federal agencies concerned with transportation (including consultants)	X			X	X	X
Review of past major studies (issues) to identify unmet needs		X				X
Public hearings		X				X
Comparison of public goals with allocation of funds among modes			X			
Comparison of public goals with carrier trends						X

Report in 1949 was prepared at the request of President Truman; and, the 1951 Doyle study was carried out by a Senate subcommittee.

Once established, the various study groups tended to identify issues based on their perception of current transportation problems. Generally, the congressional or presidential mandate indicated a broad study area, such as public aid (BIR) or coordinated federal programs (Sawyer Report). As shown in table 5-1, specific issues were derived by conducting public hearings, reviewing past studies (issues), comparing public goals (assumed) with the allocation of federal funds to various modes, and comparison of public goals with carrier trends. None of the six major studies identified above appeared to expand on the conclusions from prior research, and in fact it was rare that previous research, with the exception of the Coordinator's Reports, was referenced. In the few instances where historic research was mentioned, the result seemed to be a repetitive identification of issues, rather than an acknowledgment that such issues still existed, accompanied by more sophisticated analysis.

Table 5-2 compares the issues identified among the six major transportation studies. Issues are segmented into four broad categories: (1) economic regulation, (2) carrier problems and needs, (3) federal promotion/aid, and (4) other, which represents a combination of the above and several basic Goal Issues. Economic regulatory issues are ubiquitous and exist simply because outside controls are superimposed on an intricate market system. As previously indicated, once regulators have to determine market prices, entry and operating magnitude, merger appropriateness, and service levels, among other economic factors, a seemingly endless array of questions arise as to the criteria, data requirements, administration, and impact of such public decisions. Thus, it is not surprising to observe in table 5-2 that carrier rate-making has been identified as a major issue in five of the six major studies—the lone exception being the BIR study, which focused solely on public aid. It is also interesting to note from table 5-2 that in the past two decades entry criteria have been a popular subject, with stress toward liberalization of entry restrictions of motor common carriers. This subject was excluded from earlier studies for rather obvious reasons. Motor carriers were not regulated until 1935, and it was not until well after World War II that any semblance of regulatory criteria could be ascertained. The first major effort after the war period, the 1949 Sawyer Report, raised the possibility of entry reform, and this issue has reoccurred in every significant regulatory study since that time. There are virtually hundreds, if not thousands, of specific regulatory issues, but, as shown in table 5-2, they tend to fall under the major headings of rates, entry (including operating rights), mergers, safety, and other—the latter including a host of subjects such as service abandonment, enforcement, and cost ascertainment.

Many issues identified in the six major studies are synonymous with carrier problems and/or needs. For instance, table 5-2 shows that "aged and surplus rail facilities" was identified as a major issue in almost all of the studies. In fact, most carrier problems, tended to be rail problems—that is, passenger deficits, taxation, freight-car shortages, and labor featherbedding. Motor carrier problems tended to be highway oriented, and only a few problems of other modes were identified. The Doyle Report discussed all the issues listed in table 5-2, and more, representing in its time the most comprehensive coverage of any study on national transportation policy.

Related to both regulation and carrier needs, the six major studies also addressed federal-aid issues. Table 5-2 shows that while some studies discussed the scope of public subsidization of transport, inequitable traffic distribution and user chargers were as popular. The subject of urban transportation was raised in the two latter studies (Mueller-1960 and Doyle-1961), as was rural transportation.

Finally, an array of other, or miscellaneous, issues were identified, as presented in table 5-2. Several of these subjects were Goal Issues: national defense and inflation. One issue was the broad subject of regulatory/promotional conflicts, while other issues included the need for intermodalism, and labor-management relations. The list of so-called other issues in table 5-2 is not all-encompassing, but simply represents a sample of such issues identified among the six major studies. The sample, as with the universe it represents, is characterized by a list of issues where identification required little research. Identified issues tended to be those questions raising from the criteria (on lack of criteria) the federal government applied to regulate or promote transportation, as well as carrier needs relative to the availability of subsequent public aid.

Table 5-3 presents a comparision of recommendations among the six major transportation studies. As shown in table 5-3, four broad recommendations stand out: (1) reform regulation; (2) consolidate federal agencies promoting and/or regulating transportation; (3) broaden the federal role in transportation planning, organizing, and control; and (4) adopt user charges where they do not exist, and maintain and study existing charges. Recommendations for regulatory reform centered on two popular positions. First, regulatory balance is needed; this was usually interpreted to mean that either some of the more restrictive controls on railroads should be lifted, or that other nonrailroad modes should have increased regulation to match that of railroads. Second, the latest four studies recommended that freight rates be based on costs so that various forms of discrimination would be eliminated from the regulated transportation sector It is interesting to note that only the two Department of Commerce studies (Sawyer-1949 and Mueller-1960) suggested the potential benefits of motor-carrier deregulation, as even the later 1961 Doyle Report called for a strong, regulated common-carrier system.

An area of almost universal agreement was in the recommendation that the federal role in transportation be consolidated. While some studies did not mention DOT by name, all recommended that a single national agency be responsible for promoting transportation. Furthermore, all discussed the need for additional planning and left the explicit message that such planning should be coordinated on a national level. Three of the six studies called for a single regulatory agency, most likely the ICC, to regulate railroads, motor carriers, water carriers, and airlines. The latest four studies went a step further and suggested a broad program of coordinating regulation and promotion. The Doyle Report even called for the establishment of a joint congressional committee on transportation to encompass all modes, terminals, and related matters. In essence, the clear and strong direction emanating from the aggregation of major research studies was that transportation policy, planning, and procedures should be centralized at the national level. This trend is consistent with the other recommendation under the consolidation category outlined in table 5-3—of developing a national transportation defense policy (that is, a Goal Issue).

Aside from regulatory reform and a consolidated federal role, table 5-3 shows that a broadened federal role in transportation was generally supported by the six studies. In the earlier Planning Board study (1942), related recommendations came in the form of developing a national rail merger plan, constucting a national system of highways, subsidizing railroads, giving the federal government the right of eminent domain, and developing a national system of airports. In later studies, many of these recommendations were supported, and added to the list were such items as increasing federal data-collection efforts (including a Census of Transportation), and developing a rail passenger corporation. Relative to the number of regulatory recommendations which remain contemporary and thus have induced little, if any, action, all of the recommendations in table 5-3 under the classification of a broader federal role have been fulfilled—the latest being a national rail merger plan as developed by the Rail Service Planning Office of the ICC.

Finally, the latest five of the six studies recommended the implementation of waterway user charges, and the latest three reports made a similar recommendation for air carriers. Since motor carriers already were paying highway user charges, three of the studies suggested that such fees be continued and/or studied to determine a "fair" method of assessment. Although user charges may fall under the classification of being a subject of economics, implementation of such charges brings the federal government further into the transportation community. The methods of determination, collection process, and control of user charges, would all be subject to federal administration.

In summary, there is strong reason to believe that policy research has supported, if not led, the trend toward increased federal involvement in transportation. Three underlying characteristics of past major research studies appear to accompany the reliance on national solutions to variable problems.

First, the root problem of political (regional) parochialism has been ignored in favor of addressing conflicts among economic and social goals. Rather than focusing on the understandably unpopular subject of how regional desires adversely affect national interest, much transportation research has addressed the identification and analysis of trade-offs among economic efficiency and social

Table 5-2
Comparison of Issue Identification among Six Major Transportation Studies 1942-1961

Major Issues Identified	1942 Planning Board	1944 BIR	1949 D-O	1949 Sawyer	1960 Mueller	1961 Doyle
1. Economic regulation						
rate-making	X		X	X	X	X
entry criteria (esp. trucking)				X	X	X
safety				X	X	X
mergers (especially rail)					X	X
other economic reg.				X	X	X
2. Carrier problems/needs						
inadequacy of terminals	X					X
aged and surplus rail facilities	X		X	X	X	X
street/road upgrading	X					X
merchant marine					X	X
rail passenger deficits					X	X
taxation of rail		X				X
shortage of rail freight cars						X
small-shipment deficits				X		X
rail-labor featherbedding	X					X
airline overcapacity			X			X
3. Promotion/aid						
inequitable traffic distribution	X			X		X
extent (misallocation)		X	X			X
users charges		X	X		X	X
urban transport					X	X
rural service						X
corruption			X			
4. Other						
national defense				X	X	X
regulatory/promotional conflicts				X		X
need for intermodalism						X
labor-management relations						X
inflated prices	X					

Table 5–3
Comparison of Recommendations among Six Major Transportation Studies, 1942–1961

Major Recommendations	1942 Planning Board	1944 BIR	1949 D-O	1949 Sawyer	1960 Mueller	1961 Doyle
1. Regulatory reform						
regulatory balance	X		X	X	X	X
dev. cost-based rates			X	X	X	X
consider deregulation (especially truck and air)				X	X	
2. Consolidation of federal role						
promotion (establish DOT)	X	X	X	X	X	X
regulation (one agency)		X	X			X
improve planning	X	X	X	X	X	X
coordinate regulation and promotion			X	X	X	X
form joint Congressional committee on transport						X
develop defense policy				X	X	X
3. Broaden federal role						
national rail merger plan	X		X			X
develop national system of highways	X					
subsidize railroads	X					
Federal authority for eminent domain	X					
acquire more data (Census of Transportation)	X				X	X
develop national system of airports	X				X	
develop rail passenger corporation (public)						X
develop road classification system		X				
4. User charges						
more carriers (study and/or continue)		X	X			X
implement waterway		X	X	X	X	X
implement air				X	X	X

benefits, and, as discussed in Chapter 3, cost-benefit analyses are at best shallow. This is not to say that the latter evaluation has no validity, but its supplementation for the regional-versus-national conflict results in the single-minded solution to expand and centralize government control of transportation. After all, transportation policy involving economic efficiency, air pollution, noise, city blight, energy, etc., could seemingly best be made by a public body vested with broad responsibilities and the ability to make decisions giving proper consideration to all affected areas of concern—that is, the so-called "systems approach" to management.

Second, rather than accepting the premise that public benefits accruing from competition may be accompanied by individual risks (and harm), much transportation research appears to accept equity as a national goal, and thus focuses on ways and means to achieve transport "balance" and "coordination." Thus, many transportation studies take a carrier, rather than user, perspective. Carrier desires become synonymous with transportation problems, issues, and/or national interest. Obviously, since carriers cannot alleviate their own problems (that is why they have needs), the federal government is viewed as the logical candidate for rescuing the various modes.

Third, even where the user perspective is taken, the economic principle of value is ignored in favor of the alleged national-interest need of cross-subsidization. Little historic research has focused on what the base transportation system would be like if all forms of movement were first, on a strict pay-as-you-go structure, and second, on the basis of the federal government's providing the capacity (for example, roads, rail track, airways, rivers, etc.), but privately owned and operated transport modes using the public rights-of-way. Instead, much research centers on providing greater transportation service financed by nonusers and, in fact, nonlocal residents. Again, rhetorically speaking, who else but the federal government can best decide which groups of consumers, and locations, should cross-subsidize various other groups and locations?

In essence, all three of the above characteristics emanating from historic policy research result in a philosophy of protectionism. As shown in table 5-4 below, within each of the three conclusions, a root issue is avoided, a surrogate issue is addressed, an interest group is protected, and recommendations are made to increase federal aid.

The following sections of this chapter demonstrate the problems created by public control of transportation activities. One regulatory and one promotional case study are presented, and the concept of protectionism (that is, equity) is shown to be synonymous with the recently coined term of "do-no-direct-harm."

Immersion of Government: Case Studies

It has long been accepted by those involved in programs of federal aid that what the government helps, the government helps control. The inequities and related

Table 5–4
Impact of Issue Avoidance

Root Issue Avoided	Issue Addressed	Protected Party	Recommendation for Federal Involvement
Political parochialism	Economic-social trade-offs	Geographic regions	Consolidate regulatory and/or promotional agencies
Risk side of competition	Carrier needs	Carriers	Increase magnitude of aid
Economic value	Cross-subsidization	Users	Widen scope of coverage

problems of creating national standards for across-the-board application have been discussed in Chapter 3. Yet, government regulation and/or promotion means much more than ineffective decision criteria. It means the establishment of institutions for planning programs and delivering assistance, and thus the eventual development of a public-private marriage which is often self-serving and protective of the status quo. Charles L. Schultze, Chairman of the Council of Economic Advisors, has entitled this latter phenomenon the do-no-direct-harm principle.[1] This principle states that while "incomes and property values are constantly being created and destroyed in the normal course of economic changes that characterize a dynamic economy," government actions to achieve efficiency "are often precluded because of a fear of some direct losses."

What Schultze concluded about our society in general is analogous to that transportation environment in particular: (1) an increasing number of decisions about individual economic equities were being transferred from the market to government, (2) public policy relies too much on the application of general rules to individual circumstances, (3) government can be identified as causing losses where it has the decision-making responsibility, and (4) where government has control, it often avoids efficiency moves because of the fear of being blamed for losses. He concludes that the application of the do-no-direct-harm rule "yields an output-oriented, command-and-control approach to social intervention which is not only inefficient, but productive of far more intrusive government than is necessary."

The transportation infrastructure is glutted with examples and reflections of the do-no-direct-harm principle. All too often government has extended a seemingly helpful hand to transportation enterprise only to find itself deeply immersed in all aspects of the operation, and blindly defensive about the institutional framework developed in support of such deep-rooted involvement. Two examples of this phenomenon are presented below: (1) a regulatory example exemplified by the federal government's attempt to establish revenue-need (profit) criteria for motor carriers, and (2) a promotional example involving public attempts to develop an intercity rail transportation.

Regulation: Motor Carrier Revenue Need

During the years immediately following the Motor Carrier Act of 1935, the ICC was primarily involved in bringing stability to the trucking industry by ending rate wars. In several cases, the commission refused proposed rate reductions on the grounds that no evidence was provided to show the cost of service. Then, responding to the first attempt by a motor carrier rate bureau to increase rates, the ICC adopted the 93 percent operating ratio as the profit criterion.[2] While giving no explanation for the choice of the 93 percent figure, the commission based its rationale for adoption on the premise that trucking was a low fixed-investment industry and therefore the principal risk was more related to operating cost than to fixed investment.[3] However, the Commission ignored the fact that the ratio was not a measure of profit because it did not measure the return to the capitalist, and it did not account for interest expenses and other so-called nonoperating income and expenses. During the next ten years (1943–1953), the 93 percent operating ratio was applied in a number of cases. Although the ratio was again used in a 1953 case, a dissenting commission's opinion expressed the viewpoint that there was "too much reliance . . . on the mathematical formula of operating ratios."[4] However, the ratio was maintained in other cases through 1963.

In 1964, the commission broadened its scope of analysis by issuing an order requiring carriers not only to calculate the operating ratio but also the ratio of net operating income to net depreciated investment plus working capital (return on investment), and the ratio of net profit to shareholders' equity (return on equity). The order also detailed requirements for determining the sample of carriers to make up the so-called representative carriers proposing rate increases. For the next few years, proposed rate increases were refused in seven straight cases because the ICC deemed the carrier sample to be nonsupportable by statistical evidence. The measure of profit was not an issue in any of these cases. Finally, a U.S. District Court directed the commission to "explain what type of data" it required.[5]

The year 1967 marked a radical change in the ICC's attitude toward determining revenue need, moving the commission toward the cost-of-capital issue. On April 28, the so-called "Big Order" was issued, stating that the carriers should

produce evidence of the sum of money, in addition to operating expenses, needed to attract debt and equity captial which they require to insure financial stability and the capacity to render service.

Following the Big Order, the profit criteria became increasingly vague, inconsistent, and still lacking in support. In several cases, the ICC refused to allow rate increases because the cost of capital was not even estimated. While also refusing a rate increase in a 1969 case, the commission indicated, but did not explain why, a 10 percent return on equity would be the minimum profit needed.[6] However, in another 1969 case, it refused an increase because a 26 percent return on investment was thought to be unjustified.[7] Then, in a subsequent case, the commission approved the rates because the bureau had lower returns than the motor carrier industry as a whole.[8] Going even further, in another case the ICC approved rates because a bureau's returns were below the averages of manufacturing companies.[9] But the commission then reverted back to a prior unsupported rationale by approving rates simply because the overall return on equity was under 6 percent.[10]

In both 1970 and 1971, all motor-carrier bureau attempts to increase rates were approved without litigation. The commission's investigation of revenue-need criteria during 1970 (Ex Parte No. MC-82) resulted in an order which essentially called for the same three alleged measures of profit, and a few additional financial ratios to be calculated. While MC-82 demanded more comprehensive and sophisticated data than previously required, no clues were provided as to how such data would be used. Also, none of the financial ratios were interrelated so as to indicate the level that those standards should be at in order to assure adequate capital. Then in 1975, Ex Parte No. MC-92 required additional data on traffic, cost, owner-operators, and, above all, monthly funds-flow statements.

Figure 5-1 traces the proliferation of motor carrier revenue-need data required by the ICC. Required data has increased at an accelerated rate and touches a myriad of carrier operating and managerial functions—traffic flows, financial indicators, cost measures, sampling, and funding methods, to name a few. Yet, the commission still has no explicit and consistent revenue-need criteria for motor carrier application.

Despite what might rightfully be categorized as a deficiency, the ICC is not solely to blame for the lack of revenue-need criteria. Determining needed revenues is an economic issue which spans the horizon of microeconomics. Earnings requirements depend on a host of interrelated factors comprising a circular logic with no discernible beginning. For instance, revenue need depends on investment levels which, in turn, are a function of operating costs, methods of financing, the cost of capital, and demand elasticities. Conversely, investment levels are a function of earnings which likewise depend on cost-price-demand relationships.

The circular linkage of investment, cost, financing, pricing, demand—ultimately profit—is depicted in figure 5-2. The interrelationships of profit determinants are evident in even the most simple instance. Consider the trucking executive, who, in trying to determine his so-called revenue need, plays out the following oversimplified scenario: "The number of new trucks I have to buy

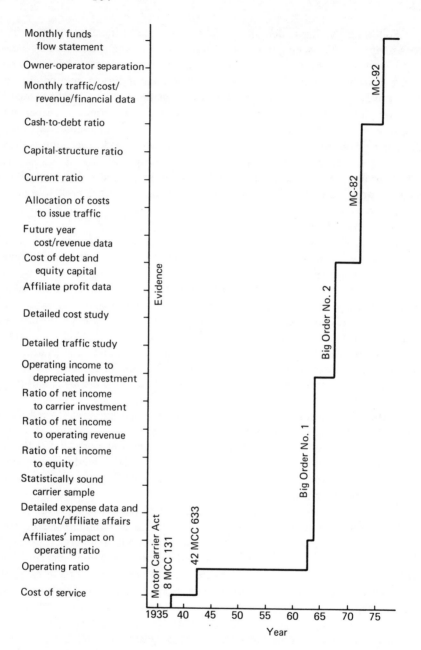

Figure 5-1. Earnings Evidence Required from Motor Common Carriers by the Interstate Commerce Commission

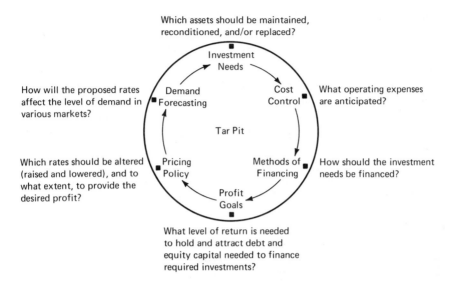

Which assets should be maintained, reconditioned, and/or replaced?

How will the proposed rates affect the level of demand in various markets?

What operating expenses are anticipated?

Which rates should be altered (raised and lowered), and to what extent, to provide the desired profit?

How should the investment needs be financed?

What level of return is needed to hold and attract debt and equity capital needed to finance required investments?

Figure 5-2. Circularity of Issues Relative to Determining Revenue Needs

depends on the competitiveness of my rates; rates have to cover costs, including the cost of capital, but this latter cost depends on profit; yet, my profit depends on how many trucks I buy." A number of factors have been left out of the preceding example including methods of financing, productivity, and, of significant importance, investment risk. Still, the message is evident. Revenue need is an economic issue which reflects the comprehensive interaction of supply and demand—that is, the free market system. Any attempt to regulate the entire network of factors affecting motor-carrier earnings would lead to what Professor McKie calls the "tar-baby effect"—that is, a situation where the regulation of any factor leads to additional regulation of other factors until a point of "indefinite extension of control" is reached.[11] Based on recent trends, it appears that public policy may have already reached the stage where decisions are being made within the "tar pit."

Promotion: Commuter Rail Service

To those not familiar with the scope and depth of federal intervention in transportation, commuter service by railroad (heavy vehicle) would appear to be strictly a private and local matter. After all, a strong case can be made for keeping such service within the private sector because of available, and often competing, public services such as bus operations, trolleys, subways, electric light-rail lines, and various forms of subsidized para-transit. Similarly, commuter service is logically a local endeavor because it directly benefits those using the system. However, just as the federal government came to the aid of local transit through the Urban Mass Transportation Act of 1964 and amended provisions, recent legislation has moved the government into the position of subsidiary rail commuter aid. Such subsidization is accompanied by a set of controlling features which may not only be counterproductive but which may undermine the very service they were supposed to retain, maintain, and improve.

Rail commuter service is very much alive in this country. As shown in table 5-5, about 34.2 million train-miles of such service were provided in 1976. ConRail (Penn Central, Reading, Erie Lackawanna, and Central of New Jersey) accounted for slightly more than half the service. Major rail commuter centers are Philadelphia (ConRail), New York (Long Island Railroad), Boston (Boston & Maine), and Chicago (seven railroads). The Philadelphia area probably enjoys the most comprehensive commuter rail service in the country and provides a good example of the problems and inconsistencies inherent in federal aid.

Table 5-5
Passenger Train-Miles of Railroads Providing Commuter Service, 1976

| Railroad | Train-Miles (thousands) | | |
	Locomotive	Motor Car	Total
Penn Central[a]	2,488	8,408	10,896
Long Island	1,791	5,666	7,457
Reading[a]	29	2,824	2,853
Erie Lackawanna[a]	972	1,532	2,504
Chicago & Northwestern	2,479	–	2,479
Boston & Maine	–	1,518	1,518
Illinois Central Gulf	19	1,489	1,508
Milwaukee	1,007	–	1,007
Central of New Jersey[a]	566	404	970
Chicago, Rock Island & Pacific	787	–	787
Burlington Northern	717	–	717
Southern Pacific	637	–	637
Chessie (B&O)	122	225	347
Chicago S. Shore & S. Bend[b]	300	–	300
Grand Trunk Western	156	–	156
Norfolk & Western	27	–	27
Total			34,163

Source: Annual Report of Carriers to Interstate Commerce Commission. Figures from Chicago S. Shore & S. Bend based on discussion with controller.

[a]First-quarter figures multiplied by four (taken over by ConRail in 1976).

[b]Do not report train-miles. Figure estimated based on 1.8 million car-miles divided by six.

Section 304(e) of the 3-R Act established a program of federal aid to rail commuter lines, beginning at 100 percent subsidy (six months), and eventually reducing to 50 percent. Funds were to be distributed by UMTA under Section 17, "Emergency Operating Assistance," of the UMT Act. Certain properties were to be conveyed to public agencies responsible for administering commuter service on April 1, 1976—the same date that the subsidy program was to begin. In Philadelphia, the Southeastern Pennsylvania Transportation Authority (SEPTA) was to receive the federal aid and pay ConRail for the cost of commuter service. At first there appeared to be only two major roadblocks to such an arrangement. First, railroads have a relatively large amount of common costs and guidelines had to be established for allocating such costs to commuter service. Second, AMTRAK owned track and facilities in the Northeast Corridor, which ConRail would have to use; this ownership barrier required another set of cost-allocation guidelines. To address these technical inhibitors, the applicable legislation stated that the Rail Services Planning Office (RSPO) of the ICC set the standards for determining continuation subsidies for commuter rail service. Furthermore, as well as containing its own labor-protective language (Title 5), the 3-R Act tied the receipt of commuter subsidies into the labor-protection clause of the UMT Act (Section 13(c), as previously discussed), concurrently requiring that the Department of Labor (DOL) approve Section 13 applications. To SEPTA, this meant that at the federal level it had to conform with RSPO cost-determination and allocation standards, UMTA planning and labor-protection provisions, and DOL labor-protection assurances. It also had to work closely with the Delaware Valley Regional Planning Commission, designated as the planning agency through which UMTA funds should be channeled to local Philadelphia-area recipients. At the same time, SEPTA was to administer the payments of funds to ConRail, which in turn subcontracted some service to AMTRAK; both of these railroads also received federal subsidies and were required to comply with safety, economic, and/or accounting regulations of the ICC, DOT, and Public Utilities Commission of Pennsylvania. Finally, since SEPTA also received state and local funds, it had to be sensitive to requirements of Pennsylvania, and local political entities comprising its board—the city of Philadelphia and the counties of Bucks, Chester, Delaware, and Montgomery. The organizational relationships within which SEPTA operates are depicted in figure 5-3. While the complexities of organizational interrelationships are too numerous to discuss for purposes of this book, two important deficiencies, if not contradictions, resulting from federal involvement are worth noting.

One massive problem attributed to the method used by the federal government to support rail commuter service focuses on the role of RSPO and its methods of cost allocation. ConRail employees who devote 100 percent of their time to commuter service in the Philadelphia region obviously represent a legitimate expense which should be billed to SEPTA. However, major controversy has focused on the problem of allocating common costs—that is, those em-

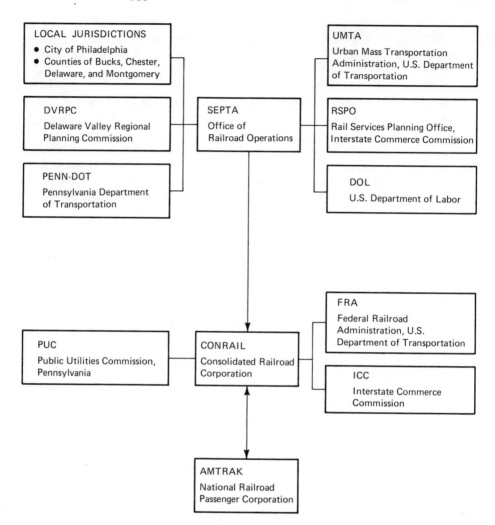

Figure 5-3. Overview of Organizational Relationships in Operation of Rail Commuter Service in Southeastern Pennsylvania

ployees, facilities, and services committed to both freight and passenger operations, or in the case of **AMTRAK**, committed to both commuter and intercity passenger travel. RSPO standards have been published, argued, revamped, argued, and refined again. Controversy surrounds such concepts as avoidable, direct, indirect, marginal, fully distributed, fixed, and variable costs. Most recently, RSPO has ordered that all common variable costs should be pro-rated to **SEPTA**, but not common fixed costs; this directive still does not address many definitional, measurement, and conceptual issues related to insuring efficient rail commuter service. Furthermore, controversy abounds over such subjects as property values (especially in regard to public purchase of previous railroad assets), reasonable returns, and measures that local public agencies (SEPTA) could use to effectively manage commuter service. What is most ironic about the millions of dollars expended in the search for "better" allocation procedures is that federal monies are involved on all sides of the issues. UMTA provides funds to SEPTA, so that SEPTA can provide funds to ConRail and AMTRAK—two federally financed railroads. In essence, it is difficult to understand why AMTRAK would charge SEPTA any amount for costs other than directly related to SEPTA service when its operation is funded by federal funds in the first place, and it would not experience a downward adjustment in costs if SEPTA operations ceased. To those who understand that cost allocation is as much an art as a science, the resources continually being used to determine RSPO-standard costs of ConRail and AMTRAK service do not appear to be worth the as yet unidentifiable benefits.

The second major problem resulting from federal intervention in rail commuter operations is the contradiction of objectives caused by labor-protection provisions accompanying aid legislation. On one hand UMTA emphasizes efficient service and threatens to hold back funds if productivity is not increased, or at a minimum if attempts are not made to operate efficiently. Yet, at the same time it enforces Part I, Section 5 of the IC Act, Title V of the 3-R Act, and Section 13(c) of the UMT Act—all stating in some form or fashion that employees cannot experience a worsening of positions due to programs and changes associated with federal funding. Thus the federal government is directing rail commuter operations to become more efficient, but not to do so in the area of labor. With the federal share of rail-commuter subsidization diminishing from 100 to 50 percent within the next few years, local communities may find themselves subsidizing wasteful labor expenses because of federal mandates. Furthermore, Section 17 (UMT Act) funding is scheduled to terminate in 1981, meaning that local public agencies such as SEPTA may be stuck with federal labor restrictions for a terminated aid program.

The implications of federally legislated, labor-protection provisions for local political jurisdictions are potentially mammoth. Railroads such as ConRail have established comprehensive labor-management systems in order to provide some form of order in dealing with the twenty or so individual unions representing rail labor. Employees are not only protected by federal legislation but have historically enjoyed detailed work-rule and seniority benefits. These institutional characteristics make it difficult, at best, for a local public agency such as SEPTA to manage effectively the maze of grievances, union negotiations, interpretations of agreements, etc., that are an implicit part of railroading. Even if SEPTA desired to take over the chore of providing rail commuter service itself (as opposed to contracting with ConRail), numerous legal questions would have to be addressed. Would SEPTA be an interstate railroad subject to ICC regulation? If it terminated its abbreviated New Jersey (Trenton) and Delaware (Wilmington) service, would it be an intrastate carrier subject to only PUC regulation? Could it possibly be classified as something other than a railroad to provide it with operating flexibility? If so, would it still have to abide by federal labor-protection provisions? Answers to these questions, and more, would probably take years of study, judicial interpretation, and possibly even congressional action. Meanwhile, SEPTA would be responsible for a rail commuter service experiencing increasing operating deficits in the face of decreasing federal subsidies. This service would operate, in some cases, alongside public bus, subway, light-rail, and trolley service. However, federal control would limit SEPTA's flexibility in making the service more economical.

Impact Diversion

One of the more revealing aspects of the relationship between transportation research policy is that recommendations for additional federal promotion have a far better chance of being implemented than do recommendations for regulatory reform. This diversion, evidenced by the increasing number and magnitude of aid programs contrasted with stiff resistance to regulatory reform, is consistent with the do-no-direct-harm principle, parochialism, and the national trend toward a more planned economy. While it is certainly clear that public decision-makers have a short-run vested interest in perpetuating central control, it is much less evident as to why the research complex has not been more vocal and had more influence in stopping an alarming trend. Some rather interesting reasons behind regulatory-promotional impact diversion can be inferred from signals gathered in the literature search (Chapter 2).

Probably the major reason for the research-policy connection summarized above (that is, impact diversion) is that regulatory reform has been marketed as "theoretical," while federal aid is sold as "practical" and "real."

Often those supporting continued economic regulation in essentially its present structure attack regulatory reformers, including advocates of deregulation, as theorists who irresponsibly cite textbook examples of perfect competition, trying to undermine the "best transportation system in the entire world." According to these protectors of status quo, perfect competition cannot exist in transportation, the government is needed to provide order, and the public is best served by carrier stability. Thus researchers addressing regulatory matters have been shadowed by a cloud of irrelevancy and, combined with the uncertainties of impacts potentially resulting from regulatory reform, their presence in ths area is somewhat futile. Yet, because researchers addressing promotional matters often conlcude that more aid is required, their views are welcomed, if not completely supported, by those protectors of present transport operators. In this latter example, an increased federal role is self-serving to both the research and carrier communities. Benefits to industry are obvious. To researchers, federal involvement in transportation means planning problems, the need for decision-making criteria, and, naturally, available research funds. It is interesting to note how "practical" it is to spend millions of federal dollars to study and plan intermodal freight systems (where it has virtually no authority to implement findings), and how "practical" it is to fund intermodal demonstration projects, AMTRAK, and ConRail. Yet, it is "theoretical" to study economic deregulation, when in fact such regulation is an unnatural state of affairs. In essence, regulation is theoretical—not the open, competitive market.

A second possible reason for the impact diversion is that conclusions regarding aid are safer than conclusions affecting regulation. Little data is required to surmise that a carrier (mode) is financially unstable; recommending initial, or increased, federal aid is logical, practical, and based on precedent. On the other hand, determining the impact of regulation requires an extensive understanding of carrier peculiarities, and available data do not approach the level needed to reach recommendations capable of gaining a consensus of support. If federal aid is increased, few individuals may be directly affected in a negative manner. However, regulatory changes can substantially alter industry structure, and even result in carrier bankruptcies. Also, researchers drawing detailed conclusions, and making specific recommendations regarding regulation, tend to get branded as either being for, or against, regulations. Within this adversary arena, research loses credibility by being prejudged. Losing credibility often results in fewer research opportunities.

Finally, researchers often choose not to "bite the hand that feeds them." DOT distributes substantial funds for transportation research, compared with a relative trickle by regulating agencies. To one receiving federal monies, the subject of the national transportation role is close to taboo. It may be for this reason that prospective contractors submit proposals to the federal government for studies that they know have already been undertaken—in part or in whole. Where money is the sole criterion of interest, federal promotion of transportation ursurps regulation. The greater the attention, the greater the public exposure, research, analysis, conclusions, recommendation, and implementation of programs and procedures.

What can be done to dissolve the research-policy relationship that leads to an unhealthy impact diversion is open to speculation. If, in fact, much research has become an arm of national policies, rather than a source of information to help lead such policies, procedures should be implemented to break this bondage. One alternative would be to strip the promotional and regulatory agencies of their research responsibilities, and aggregate transportation research, where needed, with other nontransportation research carried out by the federal government. DOT would simple serve as a conduit for federal subsidization, and the ICC, CAB, and FMC would be limited to implementing controls legislated by

Congress and interpreted by judicial review, with support of the new research entity. Another approach is to institute periodic reviews of current programs and regulations (similar to zero-based budgeting) in order to determine if historic rationale withstands contemporary conditions. Research money could be set aside for such review, whose sole purpose it would be to critically evaluate the need for continued levels of federal aid and control. Finally, aside from other alternatives not identified herein, the federal government could terminate much of its long-run research in favor of providing tax credits to those private organizations which support independent study.

In conclusion, a review of historic research studies indicates that much alleged research is not research in its precise and technical interpretation. Rather, it is unimaginative, similarly structured, predictably formed, and redundant discussion of popular issues begging the root problems which is causing increased federal involvement in transportation. This is not to say that some relevant research is not being produced. In fact, while somewhat short of analytical support and quantitative evidence, the 1961 Doyle Report can be considered a classic study (at least in the area of regulatory policies), and the overwhelming portion of its text remains applicable seventeen years later. Still, studies are continually being undertaken on issues comprehensibly covered in the Doyle Report, without even the knowledge that such a report exists. Without possession of the Doyle Report as a point of embarkation, the wheel once again gets created, and another study finds its security on the shelves in various transportation libraries. In essence, much research appears to be undertaken because funds are available, and because a supportable answer was needed for a particular question. The problem is that little attention is given to the relevancy and soundness of the question. If such focus were expressed, researchers would be encouraged to determine why so many questions are posed as the rationalization for research, when the answers to such questions will not result in changes to the delivery of improved, needed transportation services.

Notes

1. Charles L. Schultze, "The Public Use of Private Interest," Publication of the Godkin Lectures delivered at Harvard University December 1976 and published by the Brookings Institution, 1977.

2. The operating ratio is the ratio of operating expenses to operating income. A ratio of 93 means that 93 percent of operating revenues are used to pay operating expenses and 7 percent is available for interest, taxes, and accounting profit.

3. 42 M.C.C. 633 (1943).

4. 61 M.C.C. 755 (1953).

5. Ringsby Truck Lines, Inc. v. United States 263 F.S. 552 (1967).

6. 335 I.C.C. 77 (1969).

7. 335 I.C.C. 142 (1969).

8. 335 I.C.C. 185 (1969).

9. 335 I.C.C. 361 (1969).

10. 335 I.C.C. 676 (1969).

11. James W. McKie, "Regulation and the Free Market: The Problem of Boundaries," *The Bell Journal of Economics and Management Science*, Spring 1970, p. 9.

6 Concluding Thoughts

Comparative analyses of historic major research in the area of national transportation policy reflect a relatively common, and constraining, approach toward resolution of identified issues. In fact, transportation policy research has become so standardized that a profile of a comprehensive study could be hypothesized which would not be expected to deviate in any significant manner from future research. This profile would probably take a form similar to the sequence of events described within the paragraph below.

Three seemingly separate and independent events occur within a common time-span: (1) the city council of a local jurisdiction served by Metrorail commuter service in Washington, D.C., votes to withhold its share of payments for the operating deficit because of alleged service deficiencies; (2) a Chicago-based railroad announces it is on the verge of bankruptcy; and (3) longshoremen strike at West Coast ports because of job insecurity associated with containerized shipping. All three of these contrived events have a common thread. Public exposure of their existence and potential impact leads to potential engulfment and open suggestions of federal assistance. This in turn provokes declarations that the country needs an explicit national transportation policy which coordinates all facets of transportation and balances federal control and promotional programs. This theme then leads to a major study of national transportation policy, which begins with the following identification of problems:

A number of major airlines are unable to raise adequate funds in the open capital market because of dubious financial stability associated with the need for capital in the light of changing technology.

Some Midwestern railroads on the brink of bankruptcy defer maintenance to meet short-range and contractual obligations.

Motor common carriers are being forced to merge because increasing competition limits opportunities for growth and adversely affects current market penetration.

Inland water carriers are experiencing operating difficulties due to shallow channels, inadequate locks, and terminal deficiencies.

Public transit operations are facing rapidly increasing operating deficits and the self-defeating (solely in terms of ridership levels) proposition of continual fare increases.

115

State governments are concerned with the ability to finance road, bridge, and tunnel maintenance, especially as related to federally aided highways.

Other carriers are operating at either a loss, or with inadequate returns, including freight forwarders (surface and air), owner-operators of motor carriage, feeder airlines, intercity bus operators, and agriculturally exempt truckers.

Once these carrier problems are identified, they are transformed into issues within a context of federal legislation affecting public regulation and promotion. For instance, railroad financial instability is associated with improper ICC pricing constraints, improper merger criteria, and/or tight abandonment policy. Thus, corresponding issues are: How has federal regulation of rates affected adversely railroad performance? How can a national merger plan be developed to aid ailing railroads? Should the federal or local government subsidize lines which are candidates for service abandonment? Or, the plethora of regulatory issues may be aggregated simply to declare that "regulatory reform" is a major transportation issue. At any rate, where issues are identified within a framework of government involvement, resolution relies more on federal programs than on carrier ingenuity. Consequently, recommendations most often require some sort of federal action, and because impacts from such action are avoided so as not to acknowledge their severe limitations, accompanying suggestions are that more data and study are required before more specific recommendations can be made.

The profile described above is far too general and incomplete to be treated as a comprehensive model, but it does convey some of the essential characteristics of the "typical" large-scale research effort addressing national transportation policy. Existence of these research characteristics inevitably leads to further government control of transportation. In this sense, much of the transportation-policy research community has become an extension of the federal government, rather than an inquisitive advocate of the public interest seeking answers to transport problems from the user's perspective. In essence the federal government has become somewhat of an institutional barrier to the goal of economic efficiency in transportation. Furthermore, the redundancy and predictability of major transportation studies exemplifies the futility of analyses whose conclusions and recommendations are wrapped in a package of explicit caveats, disclaimers, generalities, and constant reminders of the need for further research.

It is quite obvious that major changes in attitude are needed by researchers, and those commissioning comprehensive transportation analysis, in order to develop a basic framework for policy research which explores root issues related to the role of government in transportation. These attitudinal alterations will lead researchers to wonder why DOT spends millions of dollars studying and fostering railroad-motor carrier intermodal systems when the agency has virtually no authority to implement its conclusions. New perceptions will foster a questioning of UMTA's dictating that urban transit systems be efficient while at the same time enforcing stringent labor-protection legislation. Finally, new attitudes are needed to point the finger at Congress and seek answers to questions of why legislation is passed which places regulatory agencies in the impossible position of developing and enforcing criteria which should be accomplished, and can only effectively be accomplished, by open market competition.

Changes in attitude are often more difficult to achieve than technological advancement. Still, a start in this direction is essential to effective transportation research, and eventually to the development of transportation policies truly in the public (user and nonuser) interest. The road to change should begin with a common body of knowledge which is understood, explicitly recognized, and engulfed by researchers and those responsible for developing and funding research.

Table 6-1 represents the outline of such knowledge, and is entitled "Tenets for Effective Research on Transportation Matters of National Concern." In briefly discussing each tenet below, it is the contention of this author that total absorption of the tenets, prior to issue identification and analysis, will lead researchers to ask the root questions causing misallocation of resources in transportation.

1. Transportation Is a Derived Demand. The demand for transportation derives from the demand for time and place utility. The need for products and services at specific times and in desired places creates transportation demand, and it is the user's needs and wants which should be at the core of transportation service. Research studies should be undertaken from the user's perspective so that suppliers will not be automatically recognized as fixed institutions whose welfare is of greater import than those demanding, using, and paying for the service. In this sense, identifying carrier financial problems as major transportation issues is

Table 6-1
Tenets for Effective Research on Transportation Matters of National Concern

1. Transportation is a derived demand.
2. Transportation is not a system.
3. Transportation goals are not issues.
4. Transportation policies are not explicitly stated.
5. Transportation modes are not homogeneous.
6. Transportation data are limited.
7. Transportation output is not a single factor.
8. Transportation cost-finding is an art, not a science.
9. Transportation benefits cannot be precisely measured.
10. Transportation research should recognize prior analyses.

at best secondary to focusing on the need and related user concerns, for such service. The user perspective cuts across modal lines, recognizes impact on nonusers (consumers), and does not accept federal regulations and/or promotion as fixed and needed institutions in their best interest.

2. Transportation Is Not a System. Transportation is not an entity unto itself. Although many experts refer to the "transportation system," there is often little in common between passenger and freight transportation, urban commuter service and international water carriage, and slurry pipelines and problems of owner operators. While there are some interrelationships among all things in life, and certainly there are obvious and strong interrelationships among many transportation entities, the entire transportation field itself is not one identifiable system. Consequently, consolidation of regulatory agencies insures nothing. Bringing the Federal Maritime Administration into DOT may have no impact on funding criteria. And combining regulatory and promotional agencies does not insure a "balanced and coordinated transportation system." In fact, DOT is an aggregation of a number of offices previously (before 1963) in different government agencies. Still, the FRA refers to itself as the Federal Railroad Administration, rather than DOT, and similar references are known to be popular for the FAA, UMTA, and FHWA, among others. To say that airline and railroad policies are coordinated in some incrementally effective manner is dubious to those familiar with DOT policy. Thus, organizational change and/or consolidation are/is not likely to be the panacea for serving basic transportation needs.

3. Transportation Goals Are Not Issues. It is generally accepted that transportation should be efficient, and at the same time should serve the nation's defense needs, be safe, have minimal adverse environmental impact, conserve energy, and serve all users on an equal and impartial basis. These so-called transportation goals are not issues, and the identification of them as issues creates distortions in the way research is conducted. For instance, if safety is identified as a major transportation issue, ensuing research may be limited to examining how transportation can be safer, with little, if any, regard to cost and practicality. When only one, or several, goals are thought of as issues, other goals are excluded from evaluating criteria. All of the transportation goals should be part of the evaluation criteria to be applied in subsequent research and analysis.

4. Transportation Policies Are Not Explicitly Stated. Many transportation studies conclude that the country does not have an explicit national transportattion policy and that such a statement should be developed. The 1940 Policy Statement is general and vague, and identifies goals rather than policies. Yet this does not mean that national policies do not exist. They live in every piece of legislation, every regulatory decision, and in every promotional program evident in the transportation arena. If one accepts the fact that transportation is a derived demand and not an identifiable closed-loop system, then it is reasonable to conclude that explicit policy statements cannot be effectively developed to cover the maze of activities of the federal government. Furthermore, conditions continually change, and "ad hoc" decisions made within the framework of national goals may be more desirable than those made by inflexible, written policy directions—an impossible task, at any rate.

5. Transportation Modes Are Not Homogeneous. A motor carrier is not a motor carrier is not a motor carrier. Rather, the motor-carrier industry (a loose term) consists of, among others, common carriers of general freight, specialized carriers limited to hauling one commodity (steel, refrigerated products, etc.), household goods movers, owner-operators, contract carriers, agriculturally exempt haulers, and private (industrial) transporters. Carriers range in size from small ma-and-pa operators to carriers with hundreds of millions of dollars in annual revenue. To a lesser degree, similar carrier segmentation exists for other modes. Thus, research focusing on motor carriers or, say, railroads, can be misinformed, misleading, and erroneous. Development of modal profiles is essential prior to issue identification, and certainly prior to research analysis. Research should steer away from generalities and focus on specific differences (including competition) among carriers within one mode. Transport capacity, operating characteristics, financial needs and ability, and management perspective are not homogeneous among carriers within one mode, let alone among modes.

6. Transportation Data Are Limited. Transportation data has obvious limitations because of difficulties in describing millions of combinations of people, products and geographic points. Where this fact is not recognized prior to research, the subsequent study report often states that data were too limited to draw conclusions and that additional research should be undertaken. However, inferences, conclusions, and recommendations can logically be made without the availability of all potential information, and based on data that is not perfect in each and every way (timeliness, accuracy, detail, and/or precision). Data deficiencies should be recognized prior to substantial research commitments and if at that point such data are deemed to be insufficient, related analysis should terminate.

7. Transportation Output Is Not a Single Factor. The ton-mile is often used as the single measure of output from freight transportation, while the passenger-mile holds the same position for passenger service. Both measures appear to be logical because they include both the matter being transported and the distance that freight or passengers are moved. However, while each factor may be the most descriptive single factor measuring its respective output, no single factor appropriately measures transportation service. For example, a carrier can seemingly double its productivity by producing twice the ton-miles at the same cost. However, close examination may reveal that instead of carrying feathers the carrier is now carrying gold, and its tonnage is increased substantially without changes in personnel, operations, or routes. The passenger-mile is more appropriate than the ton-mile measure because passengers are more homogeneous than freight, but a carrier produces more than a passenger traveling a specific distance. It offers capacity (seats), capacity and distance (seat-miles, bus-miles, car-miles, and train-miles), and quality of service (headways, dependability, speed, and comfort). Furthermore, passenger-miles are extremely difficult and expensive to collect, and this results in dubious application where passengers board in a geographic and political jurisdiction different from where they reside. In essence, a number of factors can be adopted to describe transportation output; researchers should consider adoption of multifactor measures so as not to reach erroneous conclusions because of definitional deficiencies.

8. Transportation Cost-Finding Is an Art, Not a Science. The determination of transportation costs requires judgment. While cost-finding can be undertaken scientifically, cost estimations can vary significantly depending on the objective of cost determination and allocation criteria to distribute common and joint costs. For instance, the cost of a railroad providing service to a grain elevator depends on whether long-run marginal (avoidable), incremental, average variable, or fully distributed costs are calculated. Furthermore, costs will depend on methods used to allocate such common costs as maintenance of way, such joint costs as empty return, and capital overhead accounts such as interest and depreciation. Cost-finding is usually undertaken in three ways: (1) accounting assignment into functional categories and subsequent allocation to work units, (2) engineering time-and-motion studies, and (3) statistical techniques such as multiple regression analysis. In some cases, all three techniques are blended, as with the ICC in cost-finding for railroads and motor carriers. However, no matter which techniques are used, and no matter how sophisticated are the program and computer in tallying both capital and operating costs, judgment is eventually required. Cost-finding has been, and remains, a controversial, scientific art.

9. Transportation Benefits Cannot Be Precisely Measured. Certain benefits resulting from any economic transaction are estimated, and transportation is no exception. Traditionally, measurable benefits include cost reduction, employment growth, and increased productivity. To the users of transportation, quantifiable benefits include rate reduction or stability, increased speed and dependability, additional capacity, etc. However, many benefits cannot be precisely measured, and even gross estimates of such impacts may be misleading. Examples of benefits not conducive to dollar estimates include better quality of service, improved safety, energy conservation, and favorable environmental impact. In view of measurement difficulties, researchers should not center their studies around cost-benefit analyses which, in reality, cannot be achieved with reliable results. Order-of-magnitude estimates are appropriate in some cases, but should not be the rule. Foolish promises of sophisticated cost-benefit analyses to rationalize comprehensive study are counterproductive and not in the best interest of the country.

10. Transportation Research Should Recognize Prior Analyses. In studying past research on national transportation policy, it was astonishing to note the avoidance of reference to prior research and analyses. The similar structure of many studies may be due to what is commonly referred to as "recreating the wheel." The conceptual arguments over many issues have been advanced repeatedly. Pinpointing of data limitations is traditional and ubiquitous. Identifying water-carrier user charges and railroad deterioration as major issues has become an expected component of policy analysis. Transportation trends are published annually by DOT and each of the regulatory agencies, and other federal agencies such as the Departments of Commerce, Agriculture, and Defense also provide transportation data. What is virtually needed is research which recognizes past analysis, data availability, and conceptual background and strives toward impact determination from alternative courses of action. Finally, alternatives should not be framed within the context that government has a responsibility to maintain present levels of service for all transport modes.

Aside from the desirability of comprehending the "Tenets" as a research prerequisite, the proposed study should be put through a rigorous test of practicality prior to the expensive tasks of research and analysis. Table 6-2 suggests such a test, entitled "Test of Practicality: Proposed Research and Analysis." This test is a series of twenty questions (actually, some questions have multiple components) which if accurately answered should result in a judgment as to the practicality of proposed study. Research may be deemed impractical for numerous reasons. For instance, an important question may be identified, but a preliminary literature search reveals that it has already been adequately answered. On the other hand, research may be desirable, but sufficient data are not available to undertake meaningful analysis. Similarly, data are available, but the organization infrastructure is not conducive to implementing recommendations. In essence, if adopted, the "Test of Practicality," combined with the "Tenets for Effective Research," should go a long way toward eliminating wasteful study, thereby providing additional funds to address root questions on the role of government in transportation.

In conclusion, both the tenets for effective policy research and the test of practicality are offered in a positive spirit. Although many tenets are stated with a somewhat negative connotation, their acknowledgment and acceptance should eliminate much unneeded and misdirected research. Furthermore, intense

Table 6–2
Test of Practicality: Proposed Research and Analysis

1. What is the overall goal of the proposed study?

2. How can this goal be transformed into a single major question which ensuing research will address? (state the question)

3. Are you identifying specific issues which, if addressed, will result in the major question to be answered? (identify issues in question form)

4. What data are needed to address issues and answer the major question? Is it available? How will you acquire such data?

5. Do you foresee certain needed, or desirable, data not being available? Why? How will such data hinder your analysis?

6. Given data availability and limitations identified in 4 and 5 above, will your conclusions withstand the scrutiny of critical evaluation by vested parties, adversaries, and public-sector decision-makers? Why?

7. What problems experienced by shippers, travelers, carriers, or other parties (including nonusers) precipitated this study?

8. What other studies have been conducted previously which directly relate to the major question of this study?

9. What conclusions have been reached in this prior research?

10. Why would you expect that your conclusions might be different from those identified above?

11. What recommendations have been reached in related prior research efforts?

12. Have previous recommendations been implemented? Why or why not?

13. Do you have reason to believe that your conclusions will have an impact on the decision-making process? If so, how? If not, why?

14. Do you anticipate that your recommendations will be implemented? Why or why not?

15. Assuming you answer the major question, who will benefit from its responsiveness? To what degree? Who might be adversely affected? How?

16. Even if your answer is responsive, supported by adequate data, well organized, etc.—in short, convincing—what action is necessary to solve problems addressed in the study?

17. How can the proposed study be used to influence decision-making?

18. How much will the proposed study cost? If the proposed research is part of a larger study program, how much will the total analysis cost?

19. Have you read, do you comprehend, and do you accept the "Tenets for Effective Research on National Transportation Policies"? If not, why not?

20. Are the expected benefits of the proposed research worth its projected costs? Why or why not?

scrutiny of the major research question to be addressed may eliminate wasteful analyses. The research community must break away from the syndrome of perpetuating federal involvement in transportation by conducting studies from the carriers' perspective, following the principle of do-no-direct-harm, and assuming that the federal government offers the only viable solutions to transport problems. A review of historic research focusing on national transportation policy and related matters—in essence, a study of studies—leads to the conclusion that such deficiencies are common. Effective transportation research demands users' viewpoints, preference for self-determination by the private sector, and realization that the public interest may require that some parties will be adversely affected by market conditions. Acceptance of the tenets for effective policy research and the test of practicality should be prerequisites to analyses. Their adoption is a first step toward focusing on the root problems of national transportation policies.

Appendix A-1
Cullom Committee Report, 1886

Reference

Report of the Senate Select Committee on Interstate Commerce, Senate Report No. 46, 49th Congress, 1st Session, 1886.

Background

On March 17, 1885, a Senate resolution established a five-man committee to investigate the regulation of transportation by railroad and by joint railroad-water carriage where control is common. This was the second congressional committee investigation of transportation—the first being the Windom Committee which recommended the establishment of a publicly owned railroad to curb railroad monopoly abuses.[a] The Committee was comprised of Chairman Shelby M. Cullom, Warner Miller, Orville H. Platt, Arthur P. Gorman, and Isham G. Harris. All five members were senators on the Select Committee of Interstate Commerce, U.S. Senate, with Chairman Cullom being from the Granger state of Illinois.

Issue Derivation

Public hearings were held before the committee. Witnesses included, among others, representatives of state regulatory commissions, carriers, and shippers—especially in the agricultural industry. The focus of attention appeared to be rate discrimination rather than rate levels. Rates had been declining rapidly prior to 1886,[b] but discrimination among products, places, and shippers appeared to be significant. In fact, the hearings were to "obtain information that will be of practical value to Congress in framing legislation for the regulation of commerce between the several states."

---

[a]*Report of the Select Committee on Transportation—Routes to the Seabord*, Senate Report No. 307, 43d Congress, 1881.

[b]D.T. Gilchrist, "Albert Fink and the Pooling System," *The Business History Review*, Spring 1960, p. 48.

Identification of Issues

1. The best method of preventing the practice of extortion and unjust discrimination by corporations engaged in interstate commerce.
2. The reasonableness of the rates now charged by such corporations for local and through traffic.
3. Whether publicity of rates should be required by law; whether changes of rates without public notice should be prohibited and the best method of securing uniformity and stability of rates.
4. The advisability of establishing a system of maximum and minimum rates for the transportation of interstate commerce.
5. The elements of cost, the conditions of business, and the other factors that should be considered in fixing the tariffs on interstate traffic.
6. Should any system of rebates and drawbacks be allowed? If so, should such transactions be regulated by law and be subject to official inspection or approval? Or should they be entirely prohibited?
7. Should pooling contracts and agreements between railroads doing an interstate business be permitted or should they be entirely prohibited by law? If they should be regulated by law, would it be sufficient to require the terms of such agreements to be made public and subject to official approval?
8. Should provisions be made by law for securing to shippers the right to select the lines and parts of lines over which their shipments shall be transported?
9. By what method can a uniform system of rates for the transportation of passengers and freight by all the corporations engaged in interstate commerce be best secured?
10. Should corporations engaged in interstate commerce be permitted to charge a lower proportionate rate for a long than for a short haul? Does the public interest require any legislation on that subject?
11. Should any concessions in rates be allowed to large shippers except those which represent the actual difference in the expense of handling large shipments over small shipments and should such concessions be made known to the public?
12. Should corporations engaged in interstate commerce be required to adopt a uniform system of accounts?
13. Is it desirable that such corporations should be required to make annual reports to the government? If so, what information as to their earnings, expenses and operations should such reports contain?
14. In making provision for securing cheap transportation, is it or is it not important that the government should develop and maintain a system of water routes?
15. In what manner can legislation for the regulation of interstate commerce be best enforced? Should a commission or other special tribunal be established to carry out the provisions of any law Congress may enact?

Conclusions/Recommendations

". . . the committee has no hesitation in declaring that prompt action by Congress upon this important subject [*sic* (regulation)] is almost unanimously demanded by public sentiment. This demand is occasioned by the existence of acknowledged evils incident to and growing out of the complicated business of transportation as now conducted, evils which the people believe can be checked and mitigated if not wholly remedied, by appropriate legislation. The committee recognizes the justice of this demand, and believes that action by Congress looking to the regulation of interstate transportation is necessary and expedient. . . ."

Appendix A-2
Moulton Report, 1933

Reference

The American Transportation Problem, prepared for the National Transportation Committee by H.G. Moulton, Brookings Institution, February 13, 1933.

Background

At the request of certain business associations, savings banks, insurance companies, and fiduciary and philanthropic institutions interested in railroad securities, the National Transportation Committee was organized to examine all phases of transportation. More specifically, the committee was to recommend a solution to railroad financial instability. Members of the committee included Chairman Bernard M. Baruch, Alfred E. Smith, Alexander Legge and Clark Howell. The Brookings study was one input to the committee.

Issue Derivation

Issues were primarily an outgrowth of the depression. Open hearings were held before the committee, studies were undertaken by investigating bodies, and research reflected in this study was conducted by Dr. Moulton.

Identification of Issues

1. Lack of uniform regulation.
2. Deregulation.
3. Duplicative lines.
4. Unprofitable services.
5. Competitive rates.
6. Consolidations.

Conclusions/Recommendations

1. Government should stop promoting competition among railroads.
2. Railroads should be allowed to earn a fair return on their investment through the publication of reasonable rates.

3. Regulatory restrictions on railroads should be reduced.
4. Regulatory jurisdictions should be extended to the entire national transportation system, but applied only to the extent necessary for public protection.

Appendix A-3
Reports of the Federal Coordinator of Transportation, 1933–1940

Reference

1. *Regulation of Railroads*, 73d Congress, 2d Session, Senate Document No. 119, 1934.
2. *Regulation of Transportation Agencies*, 73d Congress, Senate Document No. 152, 1934.
3. *Report of the Federal Coordinator of Transportation, 1934*, 74th Congress, 1st Session, House Document No. 89, 1935.
4. *Fourth Report of the Federal Coordinator of Transportation on Transportation Legislation*, 74th Congress, 2nd Session, House Document No. 394, 1936.
5. Other reports on economy projects: *Freight Traffic Report, Merchandise Traffic Report, Passenger Traffic Report, Report on Freight Car Pooling, Container Report, Report on Economy Possibilities of Regional Coordination Projects, Second Report on Economy Possibilities of Regional Coordination Projects, Railway Traffic Organization Report, Memorandum on the Application of the Clearing House Principle to the Business of the American Railways, Report on Preservation of Railroad Ties.*
6. *Public Aids to Transportation*
   Vol. I.   General Comparative Analysis and Public Aids to Scheduled Air Transportation, 1940;
   Vol. II.   Aids to Railroads and Related Subjects, 1938;
   Vol. III. Public Aids to Transportation by Water, 1939;
   Vol. IV.   Public Aids to Motor Vehicle Transportation—An Analysis of Highway and Street Costs and Motor Vehicle User Payments, 1940.

Background

The Emergency Railroad Transportation Act of 1933 (amendment to Part I of the Interstate Commerce Act) created the position of federal Coordinator of Transportation and three regional coordinating committees, each composed of five members selected by carriers and two members designated by the Coordinator. Chairman of the Interstate Commerce Commission, Joseph B. Eastman, was the federal Coordinator, supported by Dr. Charles S. Morgan, also of the commission, who supervised the research. The Coordinator's tasks were to: (1) encourage carriers to eliminate useless duplication and other waste, (2) promote financial reorganization to reduce carrier fixed charges, and (3) study means to improve transportation in general. After the Coordinator's position expired in 1936, Dr. Morgan carried on the research, funded by the ICC and National Industrial Recovery Funds from the Bureau of the Budget. Dr. Morgan's Public Aids to Transportation comprised four volumes, as identified above.

Issue Derivation

The Coordinator's reports were the first research effort based on a quantitative evaluation of the joint questions of impact from federal regulation and promotion. Rather than employing hearings, the Coordinator's staff relied on statistical descriptions of carrier performance and government involvement. The financial condition of the railroad industry had deteriorated drastically in the early 1930s and the industry had pressured Congress for solutions. The Emergency Act of 1933 responded to these conditions, and the Coordinator was provided with the responsibility of identifying specific issues. The tentative outline of reports was sent to those having expertise on the subject: federal government departments, state agnecies, carrier associations, university professors, other interest groups, and individual experts not affiliated with any of the above organizations.

Identification of Issues

Three issues initially identified were:

1. Is there need for a radical or major change in the organization, conduct and regulation of the railroad industry which can be accomplished by federal legislation?
2. Is there need for federal legislation to regulate other transportation agencies and to promote the proper coordination of all means of transport?
3. Is there need for amendments to federal statutes to improve details of the present system of regulating railroads?

Comprehensive responses to preceding questions required resolution of five other major issues as listed below:

4. *Public regulation:* Should other modes be subjected to more regulation or should railroad regulation be relaxed?

5. *Coordination:* Should public policy be geared to encouraging the development of a national transportation system in which the various forms of transportation concentrate on what they do best and less on overall competition?
6. *Public aids:* To what extent are public aids conferring competitive advantages to different transportation modes? If substantial competitive advantages exist, how can this situation be corrected, if desirable to correct?
7. *Public safety and convenience:* Should the federal government limit the dimensions, weight, and speed of motor vehicles and prescribe requirements regarding driver qualifications and insurance coverage?
8. *Labor conditions:* Is federal legislation necessary for the protection of public safety and labor beyond restricting hours of service among railroad employees, and providing a procedure for collective bargaining?

Conclusions/Recommendations

Several important conclusions were reached regarding the historical analysis of public assistance to transportation:

1. Railroads have received the largest amount of public assistance in terms of land grants, loans, etc. However, in terms of service and benefits to the nation, the aids given to the railroads are by far the most justified. The advent of railroad expansion to the west dramatically reduced transportation costs, permitted settlement in isolated areas, promoted national unity, and greatly contributed to the increase in national wealth.
2. Although the development of waterways played a pioneering role in the nation's growth, its overall impact was limited. Waterway improvements after 1900 provided cheaper service to certain shippers and sections of the country.
3. Highway improvements also realized more limited benefits than rail transport, although they lessened rural isolation, made possible a new form of transportation, created new travel habits, and, directly or indirectly, led to savings in transportation costs.
4. Finally, aids to air transportation created significant reductions in passenger travel times.

On the other hand, public aids were deemed to have created significant problems:

1. Public aids were judged inevitably to result in the provision of excessive transportation capacity which encouraged rate cutting, depleted carrier earnings, and created price discrimination.

2. Public aids to water transportation, without the existence of user charges, had a serious adverse impact on railroads while benefiting only certain shipper groups and sections of the country.
3. Highway aids also adversely impacted railroads, but the existence of user charges made this form of public assistance less objectionable.

The overall conclusion was simply stated as, "In view of the foregoing, serious consideration needs to be given to the possibilities of withdrawing or otherwise coping with the public aids now being granted and, in view of the large expenditures that appear in prospect, the means of assuring that the further granting of public aids will be subjected to close scrutiny to find what they offer of public advantage."

Recommendations fell into three major categories:

1. A proposed bill for regulating water carriers under the ICC, consisting of the following:
   a. Control over amount of complete service offered to guard against excess capacity.
   b. Control over minimum and maximum charges to prevent destructive competition.
   c. Control over operations of contract and private carriers.
   d. Adherence to published schedules and prevention of unjust rate discrimination.
   e. Coordination with other forms of transportation—specifically, the establishment of rail-water through routes.
   f. Rate changes subject to ICC suspension and investigation.
   g. Requirement for certificate of public convenience and necessity.
   h. Restriction against carriers hauling their own commodities.
   i. ICC ability to prescribe commodities which contract carriers could haul.
2. A proposed bill for the regulation of motor carriers under the ICC, consisting of the following:
   a. Requirement for certificate of public convenience and necessity.
   b. ICC power to designate routes and termini between which a common carrier could legally operate.
   c. Requirement that contract carriers receive ICC permit.
   d. ICC power to approve consolidation, merger, or acquisition.
   e. Similar rate regulation as provided for railroads.
   f. Similar filing and posting requirements as provided by railroads.
   g. Requirement that contract carriers file and publish schedules and not apply rates below minimums established by ICC.
3. Recommendations to enact legislation for amendments to the Interstate Commerce Act as follows:

a.   Establish through water/railroad routes where deemed necessary, regardless of the "short-hauling" of any carrier and to enable the ICC to prescribe minimum and maximum rail-water rates.
b.   Include ports and gateways against undue preference and prejudices, as specified in the Interstate Commerce Act.
c.   Shorten the statutory periods of limitation with respect to reparation claims to one year in the case of over- and under-charges, and to ninety days in the case of all other claims.

Appendix A-4
National Resources
Planning Board Study,
1942

Reference

"Transportation and National Policy," Advisory Committee for the Transportation Study, National Resources Planning Board (Washington, D.C.: U.S. Government Printing Office, May 1942).

Background

During the 1930s, when it became apparent that the United States was headed for war, Congress granted President Roosevelt special powers to enact certain wartime emergency measures. The President formed several ad hoc agencies and committees under the auspices of these powers. One such organization was the National Resources Committee, which was created by Executive Order 7605 on June 7, 1935. Under Reorganization Plan #1, the committee was replaced by the National Resources Planning Board, which came into existence on April 25, 1939, and lasted until sometime in 1944. During its lifetime, the board acted as a central clearinghouse for information regarding national resources and published studies similar to the one under discussion on a variety of topics, including land use.

Issue Derivation

The report was written by Planning Board staff and other federal agencies concerned with transportation, including the ICC, Department of Agriculture, Maritime Commission, etc. It was reviewed by members of the Advisory Committee to the Transportation Study which also had the responsibility of study organization. The final report was not reviewed by this body because of the intervention of the war. The explicit purpose of the study was: (1) to assess current transportation problems related to each mode and to project such problems into the future and (2) to recommend solutions assuming the availability of then-scarce resources. Advanced technology was anticipated in aircraft, motor vehicles, water carriers, and railroads.

Identification of Issues

1. *The need for terminal reconstruction:* Terminals for railroads, trucking, as well as car-parking facilities, ports, and airports were considered to be inadequate.
   a. Airports were located too far from urban centers and were too congested.
   b. Truck depots were scattered about urban areas, often without regard to proximity to terminals of other modes.
   c. In general, terminals were old, too crowded, and in need of better accessibility.
2. *Inflated rate:* High rates and fares were thought to restrict the movement of goods.
3. *Modernization of railroads:* The report cited aging vehicles, track beds, light traffic lines which were no longer efficient, and aged terminals as constituting major problems.
4. *Streets and highways:* Needs included additional highway capacity and the separation of opposing traffic lanes and grade separation at intersections.
5. *Competition and the distribution of traffic:* "Each transport agency attempts to share traffic more logically belonging to another."
6. *Regulation:* Communities and regions claimed that the existing rate structure was discriminatory and deleterious to their economic development. Extension of railroad regulation to other modes was dubious. Carriers were undercutting rates below out-of-pocket expenses. Finally, lack of economies of scale in the trucking, and possibly in inland water transport, plus the obvious incentives to efficiency which result from the competition of numerous carriers, have created doubts regarding the desirability of strict control of entry into these industries.
7. *Railroad labor:* Inefficiencies were said to occur when workers were unable to perform work outside their class of service.

Conclusions/Recommendations

1, A single transportation agency should coordinate transportation planning as well as regulation.
2. Terminals should be reconstructed for greater efficiency and for the secondary effect of upgrading the urban areas in which they were located.
3. Public funds should be made available to railroads for modernization and improvement.
4. Railroad facilities should be consolidated to eliminate the lack of coordination and the "wasteful duplication" of facilities. The report recommended a limited number of railway systems moving along regional lines.

5. A plan should be developed for an interregional highway system, and the expansion of highway capacity in anticipation of the additional need for this type of facilities when the war ended.
6. Federal authority for eminent domain should be established.
7. Develop future plans for the location of airports and enhance aids to aviation.
8. A balance should be struck between "competitive forces and public controls." This could be achieved through new approaches to regulation. It was determined that the same approach to regulation as was used for railroads was inappropriate for other modes, since these had differing economic characteristics. In addition, it was recommended that the Transportation Agency "continue an evaluation of economic results of regulatory practices." The study also recommended resolution by ICC of the interregional freight rate controversy.
9. Effective labor-management bargaining without interruption to transportation services should be achieved and greater consideration should be given to providing uniform standards in social security legislation. The possibility of substituting workmen's compensation for employer liability should be considered.
10. In the postwar era, careful planning and coordination among the transportation industries should be undertaken before public funds are expended.

Appendix A-5
Bir Report, 1944

Reference

Public Aids to Domestic Transportation, Letter from the Board of Investigation and Research transmitting the Report to the Committee on Interstate and Foreign Commerce, September 19, 1944.

Background

The Transportation Act of 1940 established the first explicit statement of National Transportation Policy (preamble), and required an ensuing investigation on the subject of public aid to domestic transportation. More specifically, this study investigated the extent to which the various modes are the beneficiaries of public aids, without adequate compensation in return. A two-member Board of Investigation and Research was created (Robert E. Webb and C.E. Childe), and in late 1941 a staff directed by Burton N. Behling spent about three years collecting and analyzing data, and writing the BIR report. Because there were some points in the report requiring judgment, there were a number of instances where the two committee members disagreed. Therefore, aside from the conclusions reached by the study staff, each of the two committee members stated their own individual conclusions.

Issue Derivation

Issues were identified by three general methods. First, Congress identified the primary issue of public aid in the Transportation Act of 1940, where Title III, Part I, Section 302(a)(2) required the board: "to investigate the extent to which right-of-way or other transportation facilities and special services have been or are provided from public funds for the use, within the territorial limits of the continental United States, of each of the three types of carriers (by rail, highway, and water) without adequate compensation, direct or indirect, therefor, and the extent to which such carriers have been or are aided by donations of public property, payments from public funds in excess of adequate compensation for services rendered in return therefor, or extensions of Government credit." The board added air carriers to the list of modes to study.

141

Second, the board reviewed the Eastman studies of the 1930s (Coordinator's Reports) and referenced the stated need for further research in the field of public funding—especially in the area of measuring the level of allocation of funds among the various transportation modes and facilities.

Finally, the board held hearings during the week of June 29, 1942, where representatives from the various modes and other interest groups testified on issues and related matters. The board's staff examined and critically assessed such testimony and added their own analysis by collecting data from federal, state, and local government sources, as well as the carriers themselves.

Identification of Issues

This study was inspired by the recognition that a shift in public concern had occurred—from one of simply providing more transport facilities to one of promoting the most efficient system of transportation. The depression had the effect of revealing excess capacity (publicly funded), and now that the prospect of peace was near, the overriding major issue was how public investments and their maintenance should be paid for, whether by those who use the facilities, or by general taxpayers.

Subissues for each mode of transportation were:

1. Railroad—extent of aid:
   a. Land grants.
   b. Taxes.
   c. Rate concessions.
   d. Right-of-way grants.
   e. Other aid.
2. Motor transport aid:
   a. National conditions and needs.
   b. Functional classification system for highways.
   c. Allocation of costs.
   d. Identification of beneficiaries.
3. Water carriage aid:
   a. Cost computation and allocation.
   b. User charges.
   c. Adversities of publicly-owned terminals.
   d. Cost-benefit determination.
4. Air transportation aid:
   a. Measurement and allocation of cost.
   b. Airport aids—scheduled versus nonscheduled aviation.
   c. Civilian pilot-training program.

Conclusions/Recommendations

1. An economical and adequate system of transportation should be promoted through the establishment of a national planning and promotional agency.
2. All railroad land-grant provisions should be repealed.
3. The ICC should review existing railway-mail pay rates.
4. The Public Roads Administration should study the equity of motor vehicle user payments.
5. Each state should develop road and street classifications more uniformly consistent with relative traffic importance and differing functions of roads.
6. Promotional waterway policies should be based on economic considerations.
7. Changes in planning and administration of federal river and harbor projects are desirable:
    a. A federal transportation authority is needed to judge the economic soundness of individual projects.
    b. Multipurpose projects should be considered by the Chief of Engineers, U.S. Army, and other federal agencies.
    c. There is a need for more comprehensive traffic statistics and reviews of navigational projects.
8. Other individual recommendations (by each of the two members):
    a. Railroads should be encouraged to liquidate public loans (Reconstruction Finance Corporation).
    b. Water carrier user charges should be adopted.
    c. Increased regulation of public waterway terminals is needed.
    d. Domestic air transportation policy should be geared to developing a self-sustained industry.

Appendix A-6
First Hoover Commission
Report, 1949

Reference

General Management of the Executive Branch, A Report to the Congress by the Commission on Organization of the Executive Branch of the Government (Washington: U.S. Government Printing Office), February 5, 1949.

Background

Public Law 162, 80th Congress, July 7, 1947, established this commission to investigate the effectiveness of Executive Branch organization. Committee members were: Chairman, Herbert Hoover; Vice-Chairman, Dean Acheson; and the following members: Arthur S. Fleming, James Forrestal, George H. Mead, George D. Aiken, Joseph P. Kennedy, John L. McClellan, James K. Pollock, Clarence J. Brown, Carter Manasco, and James H. Rowe, Jr. The commission was to adhere to the following congressional guidelines in evaluating organizational aspects: (1) cost efficiency; (2) elimination of duplication, services, activities, etc.; (3) consolidating similar activities; (4) abolishing unnecessary endeavors; and (5) defining and limiting executive functions, services, and activities.

Issue Derivation

The commission divided work into twenty-four functional and departmental task forces which research work scope over sixteen months, interviewed governmental personnel, and received about 300 submissions from experienced individuals assigned to commission task forces.

Identification of Issues

Executive Branch Organization, including: span of control, lines of responsibility, duplication of activities, necessity for services, accountability, responsibility/authority, executive capability, and managerial (personnel) needs.

Conclusions/Recommendations

Conclusions

1. Executive-branch responsibility is divided and too many agencies adversely affect control.
2. Lines of responsibility are weak and broken in many places.
3. Executives lack tools to frame programs and policies, as well as to supervise effectively.
4. Federal government has not taken aggressive steps to build strong corps of administrators.
5. Many statutes and regulations are unduly detailed and rigid.
6. Budgeting process needs improvement.
7. Accounting methods need standardization and simplification, and decentralization is essential.
8. General administrative services are poorly organized or coordinated.

Recommendations

1. Create a more orderly grouping of the functions of government into major departments and agencies under the President.
2. Establish clear lines of control from President down.
3. Provide strong staffs to President and department heads, with executive freedom to organize.
4. Develop more capable administrators in the public service.
5. Enforce the accountability of administrators.
6. Permit agencies to administer for themselves a larger share of the routine administrative services, under strict supervision and in conformity with high standards.

Under the heading of "Commerce," the report recommends that many activities scattered throughout the government should be brought under the Department of Commerce, as follows:

1. Maritime functions (construction, operation, charter, sale of ships).
2. Coast Guard (then with Treasury Department).
3. National Advisory Committee for Aeronautics.
4. Promulgation of air safety regulations.
5. ICC safety matters.
6. Public Roads Administration (then in Federal Works Agency).
7. Office of Defense Transportation (then in Executive).
8. Commercial fisheries (then in Interior).
9. Munitions export control (then in State).

Appendix A-7
Dearing-Owens Study, 1949

Reference

Charles L. Dearing and Wilfred Owens, *National Transportation Policy* (Menasha, Wisconsin: George Banta Publishing Company), September 1949.

Background

This study can be viewed as an addendum to the Hoover Commission Report, inasmuch as a significant portion of the research is based on a study of federal transportation activities which the authors undertook at the request of the Hoover Commission on government reorganization. The commission requested the study because it felt that organizational problems could not be solved without first clarifying and making consistent, national transportation policy. Dearing and Owens had previously addressed policy issues, especially in the area of highway strategy, and were charged with the tasks of evaluating national transportation policy and making specific recommendations for revising policy and administrative organization. Before making recommendations, the authors (1) described the types of transportation facilities aided with public funds, (2) identified government organization for transportation aid, and (3) determined how such programs are financed. The study appears to be the first major publication in book form to address the sole subject of national transportation policy.

Issue Derivation

Dearing and Owens base their study on three primary assumptions concerning desirable policy goals. When their investigation of levels and allocation of public funds results in data and facts which are contrary to these assumptions, they conclude that national policy is ineffective. These assumptions are that (1) government assistance should be evenly divided among the transportation agencies—modes; (2) promotional programs should be systematically planned, be consistent, and exist in harmony with regulatory objectives; and (3) it is desirable to be able to explicitly identify responsibility for transportation efficiency and progress. By investigating the level, procedures, and allocation of funds among the various transportation modes, issues evolve which are inconsistent with stated assumptions.

Identification of Issues

The major issues are the consistency, balance, and systematic planning of national transportation policy. Subissues under these general headings are:

1. Overbuilding (surplus capacity) of rail lines.
2. Corruption in public financing.
3. Misallocation of water aid favoring large shippers.
4. Overextension of federal aid to highway development.
5. Adverse effects of operating subsidies on managerial efficiency.
6. Ill-advised airline expansion.
7. User charges versus general tax payments.

The report concludes that "federal activity has been marked by vague objectives, questionable methods of economic justification, narrowly conceived programming of expenditures, unsound financial policy, and defective administrative management."

Conclusions/Recommendations

1. National transportation policy should be based on sound economics, and be unified and consistent.
2. Regulatory policy should be systematically balanced among the modes.
3. Regulatory and promotional policy should be coordinated.
4. Rates should be based on true economic costs of service performance.
5. User charges should be adopted to recoup public aid.
6. Initiative and responsibility for basic managerial decisions should be restored to private firms—especially in rail rate-making.
7. Prospective railroad mergers should be more effectively reviewed by public representatives.
8. A transportation policy addressing national security is needed.
9. A Federal Department of Transportation should be established, to include rail, air, highway, and water carriage.
10. Components of the Federal Maritime Commission should be absorbed by the Interstate Commerce Commission.
11. Economic regulatory aspects of the Civil Aeronautics Board should be absorbed by the Interstate Commerce Commission.
12. The rule of rate-making should be amended to provide the private sector with more rate-making freedom.

Appendix A-8
Sawyer Report, 1949

Reference

Issues Involved in a Unified and Coordinated Federal Program for Transportation, Report to the President from the Secretary of Commerce, December 1, 1949.

Background

This report was prepared at the request of President Truman. At the time, federal transportation expenditures for all purposes reached such scope ($1.5 billion per year) as to warrant a critical reexamination. There had been little coordination among various federal programs which were administered by a number of agencies, each concerned with a limited sector of the transportation industry. Conflict between promotional and regulatory objectives became apparent. A unified and coordinated federal program for transportation was clearly needed. As a first step in this direction, the President requested the preparation of this report to be used later as a basis for discussion of those policy issues with the various agencies concerned with transportation.

Issue Derivation

Issues were identified from three sources: (a) federal agencies with a responsibility or an interest in transportation policy, who were asked to present their views during the preparation of the report; (b) three transportation consultants, Mr. C.E. Childe, Washington, D.C.; Dr. James C. Nelson, of the Washington State College; and Mr. Ernest W. Williams of Columbia University, who had reviewed the report; and (c) the Department of Commerce staff.

Identification of Issues

As clearly reflected in the title of the report, the major area of concern revolves around the conflict and inconsistency of federal transportation programs:

1. Promotional issues:
   a. Whether the promotion of air transportation has not proceeded at the expense of sea transport and vice versa.

b. Whether the promotion of navigable waterways and certain use of highways has impaired the economic health of the railroad industry.

c. Whether the federal government is obtaining adequate return for the expenditures.

d. Subsidy issues.

2. Regulatory (economic) issues:

a. Controls to protect the user:
- Inconsistency and inequality of the rate structure, a hardship particularly against small shippers.
- Rate discrimination.
- Inequitable effect of general rate increases.
- Delays in correcting discriminations.

b. Rate-making standards:
- Lack of clear and definite rate-making standards.
- Wide range between maximum and minimum rates permitted substantial discrimination between types of service, between commodities, between shippers of the same commodity, and between regions.
- Failed to promote the optimum use of transport resources since certain carriers have been permitted to conduct particular services at rates well below their fully distributed costs.
- Relatively few through routes and joint rates.

c. Control over entry into business:
- Restrictions on the operating certificates of motor carriers have resulted in:
  - Higher costs.
  - Higher rates.
  - More use of private trucking.
- Restrictions on air carriers' operation have resulted in reduced utilization of equipment.

d. The scope of regulatory authority, too much or too little?

e. The problem of inefficient operations, particularly railroad operations.

f. The large deficit incurred in the handling of small shipments.

g. The existing legislation concerned with the movement of transportation of mail does not keep up with the changing conditions in the field of surface transportation, particularly motor transport. The statute appears ambiguous in defining the authority of the Postmaster General and the ICC in regard to the transportation of mail by railroad.

3. Conflict between federal regulation and promotion:

a. Conflict between multiple regulatory agencies.

b. Conflict between federal promotion and rate regulation requires motor carriers and water carriers to maintain rates closely related to rail rates rather than to their own costs. Such regulatory actions nullify to a substantial degree the promotional activities in providing waterways and highways.

c. Conflict between federal promotion and regulatory restrictive measures which limit the right to enter business, hence, minimize the use that might otherwise be made of the highways, airways, and waterways.

4. National defense.

Conclusions/Recommendations

Measures recommended for modification of conflict are outlined below in general principle, but not in specific detail:

1. Federal promotional activities:
   a. Place the separate and noncoordinated promotional programs under centralized direction and control.
   b. Careful analysis of benefits (utility) should be made prior to provision of transport facilities.
   c. Develop a system of user charges where they do not now apply.
   d. Special subsidy programs would be warranted only on the basis of a clear finding by those directly concerned with the country's defense that the services to be subsidized are clearly essential from a defense standpoint. Wherever practicable, such subsidies might be charged to the budget of the National Military Establishment.

2. Federal regulatory activities.
   a. Eliminate the rates which are not closely related to the fully distributed cost of rendering the service.
   b. Consideration should be given to the restoration of penalties in the law for failure on the part of a common carrier to quote the proper rate.
   c. Conduct a thoroughgoing study of the standards of the regulatory agencies in regard to the filing and handling of tariffs and the effect of present practices upon the transport user.
   d. More vigorous action should be considered to require the establishment of economically justified joint rates and, where necessary, the law could be amended to empower the regulatory authority to require the establishment of such rates.
   e. Conduct an impact study of regulatory controls over air carriers, water carriers, and motor carriers and a reexamination of the effectiveness of regulatory controls over railroads and pipelines.
   f. Present financial controls over railroads and pipelines should be continued. In the case of other carriers where competition appears as an adequate substitution for regulation, regulatory restrictions should be held to a minimum.

g. Promote the consolidations and unifications of unprofitable services, particularly railroad, or eliminate those services. This may involve a mixture of incentives and compulsory action. One incentive requiring immediate consideration is a more liberal policy with respect to railroad abandonments.

h. Amend the present law to allow the Post Office Department to make use of the cheapest means of transportation consistent with expeditious handling of the mail.

3. Effective federal coordination.

a. Adopt the solution advanced by the Commission on Organization of the Executive Branch of the Government, that concentrates all general research and promotional activities under centralized direction and control in an agency concerned with the major questions of transportation policy, but retain separate commissions to perform essentially regulatory functions.

b. As far as subsidies are concerned, the recommended central agency might determine the overall extent of direct-subsidy programs, while the regulatory commissions would be restricted to determining which party or parties should receive particular subsidy awards.

4. Effective control of transportation in an emergency.

Any necessary wartime control agency or agencies, whatever type of organization is adopted, should be sufficiently flexible to make the most effective use of all types of transportation. To do this properly will require the relaxation or suspension of many restrictive controls on transportation, an important example of which is the easing of restrictions on motor carriers.

Appendix A-9
Mueller Report, 1960

Reference

(Report) *Federal Transportation Policy and Program*, (Appendix) *Rationale of Federal Transportation Policy*, Report transmitted to the Congress by President Eisenhower, submitted to him by the Secretary of Commerce, 1960.

Background

This report followed the President's budget message, wherein he recognized a need for comprehensive study of national transportation. Long-range objectives to be achieved within ten years included: (1) adequate capacity; (2) low cost; (3) low rates; (4) customer free choice to meet its transportation needs; (5) carrier initiative and health; (6) federal neutrality; (7) user charges; (8) reduced, or elimination of, subsidies except for defense; and (9) uniform and equitable federal economic regulation.

Issue Derivation

This report was based to a large extent on consideration of underlying studies and advice by knowledgeable consultants, contractors, and others in various fields. There were fourteen study reports prepared for the Transportation Study of the U.S. DOC. In addition to the Study Staff, others involved were: (1) Industry Advisory Groups: Transportation Council and Ad Hoc Transportation Committee of the Business Advisory Council; and (2) U.S. DOC Transportation Staff.

Identification of Issues

In nine broad areas:

1. Federal economic regulation:
   a. Control of operating rights.
      Truck.
      - Route restrictions (through gateway points).
      - Commodity restrictions.
      - Type of service restrictions.

Air
- Duplication of routes between trunklines and local service carriers.
- Schedule limitations.
- Undeveloped mass air transportation market.
- Delay in granting service permission.
- Subsidy.
- Participation of U.S. flag carriers in international traffic and capacity consultations in bilateral agreements.

   b. Control of rates.

Rail and truck.
- Competitive pricing.
- Rate-making standards.
- Long- and short-haul rates.

Air.
- Flexibility of rate-setting.
- International rates.
- Minimum rates for military traffic.

2. Federal safety regulation.
3. Cost-finding and census of transportation.
   a. Cost-finding.
- Inadequate procedures, methods, and data comparability.
- Insufficient information for intermodal cost comparisons.

   b. Lack of funding for a Census of Transportation.
4. Federal investment and user charges.
5. Defense readiness, government procurement and operation.
   a. How can the United States maintain adequate transport readiness for possible wars at reasonable economic cost for the indefinite future?
   b. Special Merchant Marine problems.
- Adequate size of the fleet.
- Construction and operating subsidies.
- The replacement problem.
- U.S. flag policy.
- International balance of payment.

6. Urban transportation.
7. Special problems.
   a. Motor carrier: uniformity of state regulation with respect to:
- Sizes.
- Weights.
- Safety appliances.

   b. Railroad.
- Passenger service deficits.
- Consolidations.

Conclusions/Recommendations

All together seventy-eight specific recommendations to resolve the issues identified above were listed. In general terms, the federal government, as recommended, should:

1. Retain sufficient basic controls of operating rights and proceed deregulation of entry gradually over an extended period of years.
2. Reduce restrictions on pricing also gradually in coordination with the program on control of entry. In the long run, rates should come to be based primarily on cost.
3. Facilitate the collection of complete and consistent cost and statistical information about all modes of transportation and provide funds for a Census of Transportation as soon as possible.
4. Continue user charge systems where they exist and establish such systems where none now exist.
5. Not operate transport systems in competition with commercial carriers if there is any other feasible way to meet minimum military requirements.
6. Encourage local authorities to do more long-range urban community planning, including total urban transportation planning to make full use of all modes to minimize total transportation cost and congestion.
7. Continue to support the Merchant Marine through subsidy to the degree necessary to maintain parity. In the long run the Merchant Marine should approach near self-sufficiency through a joint government-industry research and development program.
8. Urge the states to move rapidly toward uniform legislation with respect to sizes, weights, safety appliances, and related matters of highway vehicles operating in interstate commerce.
9. Help railroads to improve their economic situations by consolidations and abandonment of unprofitable passenger services.
10. Remove inequality in the tax treatment accorded different forms of transportation.

Appendix A-10
Doyle Report, 1961

Reference

National Transportation Policy, Report of the Committee on Commerce, United States Senate, by the Special Study Group on Transportation Policies in the United States, 86th Congress, June 26, 1961.

Background

In 1958 Congress studied the financial problems of the railroad industry, and while the four volumes of nineteen hearing sessions resulted in the Transportation Act of 1958 (amendment to the Interstate Commerce Act), it became obvious to the subcommittee that a more comprehensive study of transportation was needed before major problems could be addressed. Thus, the subcommittee recommended an eighteen-month study, employing three experts, to examine: (1) the need for regulation, (2) government assistance and user charges, (3) common ownership, (4) railroad consolidations and mergers, (5) railroad passenger service, and (6) additional regulatory and promotional matters. A research staff was employed under the direction of Major General (U.S. Air Force) John P. Doyle of Transportation Consultants, Inc., and an Advisory Council was created, including carrier, user, labor, and other transportation interest groups. Furthermore, ad hoc committees representing various interest groups were established in the areas of pricing policy, regulatory exemptions, and regulatory enforcement.

Issue Derivation

Four general methods were used to identify issues. First, some issues were dictated by Congress as a result of its 1958 investigation of railroads. Second, other issues were identified by studying transportation trends (operating and financial) among the various modes, relative to a set of assumptions identified as the "study concept." Third, issues were suggested by the study staff, the thirty-two associations, and other interest groups comprising the Advisory Council to the study staff, and the other interest groups within four ad hoc committees. Fourth, issues were collected from a multitude of books, journals, periodicals, reports, etc., reviewed by the study staff.

Identification of Issues

1. Regulation, economic.
    a. Rates.
    b. Entry.
    c. Route structure.
    d. Commodity limitations.
    e. Mergers.
    f. Acquisitions.
    g. Enforcement.
    h. Pricing.
        *   Cost-finding.
        *   Minimum-rate policy.
        *   Value of service versus cost.
        *   Long and short haul clause.
    i. Fragmented motor carrier operating certificates.
2. Regulation, noneconomic (safety).
    a. Limitation of motor carrier size and weight.
3. Promotion/financial aid.
    a. Federal aid and user charges.
    b. Future of intercity rail passenger service.
    c. Urban transportation.
    d. Public service to rural areas.
    e. Taxation of railroad way.
4. Industry structure (regulation).
    a. Common ownership.
    b. Private carriage of freight.
    c. Exemptions from regulation.
5. Need for piggyback and containerization.
6. Labor and management.
7. National rail freight-car problem—supply and cost.

Conclusions/Recommendations

1. A Joint Committee on Transportation should be created to undertake continuous studies of transportation policy, problems, and issues, and to submit recommendations thereon to appropriate standing committees.
2. The CAB, ICC, and FMB should be consolidated into a single commission having jurisdiction over economic and safety regulation.
3. A Department of Transportation should be established, to include, Bureau of Public Roads, Defense Air Transportation Administration, Federal

Aviation Agency, Maritime Administration, Office of Under Secretary of Commerce for Transportation, Panama Canal Company, St. Lawrence Seaway Development Corporation, and the National Capital Transportation Agency so long as it remains a Federal agency.

4. Lawmakers should express their intent and understanding of terms to be used in legislation. We must identify the objective—just what do we want from transportation? Are we to consider the national interest predominant or are individual interests in conflict therewith to be favored?

5. User charges should be accepted now for gradual application to air and waterway transportation over a period of years.

6. Ownership of one mode by another should be permitted to all modes equally when clearly determined in each case to be in the public interest.

7. Powers of the regulatory agency in regard to through routes and rates should be strengthened and users should be permitted to initiate applications for combination service.

8. Detailed railroad consolidation policy should be developed by the proposed Department of Transportation.

9. A single rail passenger corporation operating on existing facilities over routes chosen by competent market survey is suggested.

10. Cost-related rates are recommended so that in time the long-and-short-haul-provision controversy will be moot.

11. In regard to adequate transportation in rural areas, no recommendations are made, but the dominant issue is: What policies are needed to maintain some amount of public service?

12. The following specific rules for rate-making should result in rates based on long-run marginal costs:

    a. Rate changes which result in rates that depart further from fully distributed costs than at present may be presumed to produce rates unreasonably related to costs, unless specific evidence can be presented to demonstrate that such rates are reasonably related to long-run marginal costs.

    b. The long-and-short-haul-provisions of Section 4 of the Interstate Commerce Act should be extended to apply equally to all modes. Relief therefrom should not be extended to permit meeting the competition but only when justified on the basis of cost considerations.

    c. No carrier should be required to price his services above fully distributed cost or long-run marginal cost, whichever is higher, to protect the traffic of another carrier.

    d. In cases involving intermodal competition, pricing below the full cost of providing service by one mode which forces carriers of other modes to price below fully compensatory levels shall be presumed to be unfair, unless it can be demonstrated that such prices are not below long-run marginal costs.

    e.   Divisions of joint rates should be reasonably related to the fully distributed or long-run marginal costs of all carriers providing the service, and rate policy should encourage service over routes which will minimize the total cost of providing the service.

13. A federal law should be enacted to exempt railroad and pipeline rights-of-way from state taxation. Tax laws should make it unlawful to assess property of a common carrier engaged in interstate commerce at a value which bears a higher ratio to the market value of such property than other property subject to the same property tax levy.

14. The federal government should periodically examine, on its own initiative, government transportation.

15. Section 22 (reduced) rates are not warranted and the appropriate section of the Interstate Commerce Act should be repealed.

16. Congress should empower and direct regulatory agencies to restrict private carriage to its legitimate operation.

17. Repeal of the mixing rule for water common carriers is recommended, along with simplified entry and price control of a new class of regulated bulk carriers to come into being along with repeal of the bulk exemption.

18. Continuation of exemption for certain specific water traffic is desirable. No further extention of exemptions should take place.

19. Economic and safety regulation should be enforced or the laws should be rescinded.

20. An informational clearinghouse should be established in the appropriate federal agency for collection and dissemination of pertinent enforcement data, to be combined with an existing clearinghouse, concerning drivers found in violation of certain provisions of the Motor Vehicle Code.

21. The regulatory agency should undertake a detailed investigation of the question of limitation of highway operating authorization and its effect upon national transportation costs under congressional requirement that a program of gradual readjustment be developed toward maximum efficiency of operation, while preserving service to affected users.

22. Congress should direct the regulatory agency to develop a phased program designed to eliminate restrictions upon such authorizations which increase the economic cost of motor common carrier service (that is, operating certificates).

23. For rail commutation in urban areas, the federal government should: (1) provide low-interest loans, (2) extend the time required for train discontinuance actions by three months, and (3) adjust taxes so as to prevent any local public funds for rail operation, supplied through direct payments or tax relief, from being absorbed by federal income taxation.

24. In the area of metropolitan transportation, the federal contribution should be to: (1) better coordinate the many federal programs, (2) more actively support local planning, and (3) undertake adequate research in urban development.

25. Federal guidelines for motor vehicle size and weight limitations should be followed. Heavy vehicles should bear their full share of highway costs as the public interest requires. The federal government should favor those carriers who will move goods shipped under government bill of lading in a standardized vehicle or container.

26. The Department of Transportation should be given adequate directives and authorization to provide standardization of equipment.

27. Congress should prescribe positive policy direction and necessary resources, so the executive branch can constructively aid in shaping of labor-management relationships in transportation; Congress should vigilantly examine executive implementation of established policy; Congress should critically examine the Railway Labor Act and associated legislation for appropriate revision; and the executive branch should accept responsibility of leadership to acquaint the public with facts regarding obstructive practices wherever they appear in the transportation industry.

28. The following rule of rate-making is recommended as a criterion in suspension actions: "When a protest is filed against a proposed rate which departs further from the fully distributed costs of the proponent than does the existing rate the proposed rate, should in the absence of compelling reasons to the contrary, be suspended pending investigation and decision thereon. When the proposed rate is closer to the fully distributed cost than the existing rate it should not normally be suspended."

29. No recommendations are made regarding government regulation of service, but a suggestion is made that close watch is considered essential and congressional inquiry is recommended.

30. Industry and government working together should prescribe the details of a charter for a National Rail Freight Car Corporation to be authorized by Congress after a detailed study of such a program.

Appendix A-11
Trends and Choices, 1977

Reference

National Transportation Trends and Choices, U.S. Department of Transportation, January 12, 1977.

Background

This is a comprehensive treatment of the major planning issues on the national agenda that may impact the future development of our nation's transportation. A by-product of this effort has been the identification of certain major issues facing transportation that should be the subject of public discussion. It is not intended as a plan of action, but rather a prospectus of what is possible, practicable, and in the public interest. Two considerations that will strongly affect plans for the future, from the national scale to the neighborhood level, are the availability of liquid fuels and the continuing changes in settlement patterns of our population which lie outside the control of transportation planning and policymaking.

Issue Derivation

Trends and Choices is an agenda of national transportation issues and alternative solutions. It is not intended as a plan of action, although it encompasses programs and plans that may already have the force of law at various levels of government. It is a prospectus of what is possible, practicable, and in the public interest.

This document specifically focused on what needed to be done for the future. Extensive cost/benefit analyses were excluded. Public choices have been identified for future discussion:

1. How should available resources be allotted between present needs and long-term prospective problems?
2. When is it appropriate for the public to intervene in marketplace decisions?
3. How can government institute orderly procedures to make necessary changes in public policies?

Identification of Issues

This document addresses the future of both domestic and international transportation from 1976 through the end of the twentieth century. It covers all vehicular modes and discusses oil, gas, and slurry pipelines as well. Emphasis is on the effectiveness of U.S. international and domestic transportation, including environmental, energy consumption, and safety effects. The following list is an identification of major issues as derived from the report's focus in various areas:

1. Intermodal trade-offs.
2. Need for broad national goals and objectives in transportation.
3. Impact analysis.
4. Data requirements.
5. Correlation between private and public sectors.
6. Comprehensive planning.
7. Federal land-use policies.
8. Regulatory reform.
9. 55 MPH speed limit.
10. Truck size and weight limitations.
11. Investment criteria.
12. Evaluation criteria.

Conclusions/Recommendations

Three scenarios were presented for transportation between now and the year 2000: success, distress, and transformation.

1. In the success future—energy requirements will grow at 3 to 4 percent per year, which underscores the need for development of coal resources, shale oil, outer continental shelf oil and gas, nuclear energy, and other substitutes for liquid petroleum, along with continued large imports of foreign petroleum.

2. In the distress future—energy supply falls short. Climatic changes reduce drop production moderately and agricultural exports sharply. The overall picture is that of a recession in the 1980s deepening into a severe depression in the 1990–2000 period. Either conditions will improve or the society will be severely threatened in the post–2000 period.

3. Transportation future—envisions energy needs being satisfied by a relatively slow increase in capacity (2 percent to the year 1985 and 1 percent per year to the year 2000).

Some patterns emerged across all three scenarios:

1. Bulk commodities increase their share of total ton miles about the same, regardless of conditions.
2. A similar pattern exists for passenger transportation demand.
3. There appears to be no market for new advanced intercity transportation systems other than those essential in overcoming massive changes in energy form used.

In other conclusions, this report calculated that the transport system could not readily absorb a petroleum shortage greater than 10 percent. Emergency rationing plans are in the final stages of development. For planning purposes, it was assumed that U.S. forces were engaged in a two-front conventional war. In this scenario, an increase of less than 6 percent in ton-miles of intercity freight was anticipated. However, the national transport system, particularly the railroads, would have to be in better physical condition. The underlying theme in this study was that perhaps we will not learn so much to do new things as to do well those things we now do rather poorly.

Appendix A-12
Magnuson Committee
Report, 1977

Reference

Interstate Domestic Transportation System for Passenger and Freight, Committee on Commerce, Science and Transportation, U.S. Senate, May 1, 1977.

Background

In the late 1960s and early 1970s many research studies attacked traditional regulatory institutions. Some regulatory agencies responded by claiming that they were understaffed and underfunded. Thus, in order to address this controversy, in 1975 the Senate passed a resolution to define issues, problems, policies, and related questions regarding regulation. The Committee on Government Operations addressed regulatory issues in nontransportation areas while the Magnuson Committee focused on transportation. The original report was written by Harbridge House, a management consulting firm. Following its submission, it underwent numerous reviews by government agencies, including the White House. Data in support of this report were provided by government agencies, including the Library of Congress.

Issue Derivation

Issues were formulated after broad review of the literature, and an examination of suggestions by individual consultants supplementing the study staff. Issues were identified within modal classifications, and a number of contemporary research studies are referenced.

Identification of Issues

1. Freight
    a. Railroad
        - end-to-end vs. parallel mergers
        - abandonments
        - federal standards for plant rehabilitation
        - electrification
        - rate structure inconsistencies and criteria

    b. Motor carrier
        •   regulatory constraints
            —inefficiencies caused by certificates
            —lack of competition
        •   highway user charges
        •   size and weight restrictions
    c. Air—deregulation
    d. Waterway
        •   operating needs
        •   environmental impact
    e. Coal slurry pipeline
        •   effect on competition
        •   water consumption, energy use
    f. Government role in advancing intermodalism
2. Passenger
    a. Railroad
        •   route structure
        •   service standards
        •   impact of subsidies on bus operations
    b. Highway
        •   maintenance
        •   level of federal aid
    c. Bus—deregulation
    d. Air—deregulation
    e. Intermodal

Conclusions/Recommendations

1. The federal government lacks a coherent regulatory policy.
2. Consideration of the impact of railroad electrification should be included in determining a national energy policy.
3. Complete research of the implications of the 3R and 4R Acts should be undertaken.
4. Improve railroad branch-line treatment including cost-reducing reforms such as containerized cargo and coordinated truck-rail service, restructuring of freight rates, reduction of crew size, conversion to independent short-line railroads, and public subsidies to branch lines.
5. Further study of railroad rate regulation legislation is necessary.
6. Additional research is needed on truck size and weight restrictions.
7. Congress must make the decisions regarding improvements of inland waterways and should consider proceeding with such a project very carefully.

8. More analysis is needed regarding competition between coal slurry pipelines and railroads.

9. Because of the substantial costs involved, additional study should be undertaken regarding expansion of rail passenger service.

10. Since the federal highway program is at a transitional stage, further study should be undertaken to establish national policy.

11. Recommendations for bus transportation are: (1) smaller buses on more remote routes and at off-peak hours should be market tested, (2) charter and special service should be promoted, (3) suburban bus stations should be used as well for intermetropolitan transportation, and (4) interiors of buses might be redesigned to provide more comfortable seating arrangements.

12. Significant intermodal transportation can be achieved through better urban access to intercity common carriage.

Appendix B-1
Congressional Hearings on
Transportation, 1887-1932

Year	*Title*
1899	Relating to Transportation
1900	Government to Take Control of Transportation
1904	Regulation of Rates, Railroads
1904	Amend Law Relating to Interstate Commerce
1904-1905	Relation of Railroad Rates
1907	Railroad Passenger Fares and Mileage Tickets
1908	Railroad Passenger Fares and Passengers
1908	Railroad Freight Rates and Routing Shipments
1910	Railroad Rates, Court of Commerce
1911	National Waterways Commission
1913	Classification of Freight
1914	Gas Pipelines to Make Common Carriers
1916	Discrimination of Common Carriers
1916	Bills Affecting Interstate Commerce
1916	Regulation of Interstate Rates
1916-1917	Transportation
1917	Creation of a Committee on Aeronautics
1918	Inland Waterway Transportation
1918	Relinquishment of Control of Railroad System
1918	Federal Operation of Transportation Systems
1919	Utilization of Inland Waterway Transportation
1919	Appropriation for Federal Control of Transportation System
1920	Amend Merchant Marine Act
1920	Extension of Tenure of Government Control Railroads
1920	Transportation Shortage: Railroad
1920	Transportation Act
1920	Complete System of Connecting Lake Erie with the Ohio River: Waterways for the United States
1921	Civil Aviation in the Department of Commerce
1921	Extension of Government Guaranty to Carriers by Water
1921	Railroad Funding Bill
1921	Railroad Revenues and Expenses
1921	Transportation Act, Amendment Relating to Partial Payments to Railroad
1921	Modification of Transportation Act, 1920

Year	Title
1922	Canals, Rivers, and Harbors
1922	Amendment of Paragraph 15 of Section 1, Interstate Commerce Act
1922	Railroad Revenues and Expenses
1922	Proposed Amendment of Transportation Act of 1920
1923	Relating to the Carriage of Goods by Sea
1923	Law Memoranda upon Civil Aeronautics
1924	Bureaus of Civil Air Navigation, etc.
1924	Inland Waterways Corporation
1924	Railroad Rate Structure
1924	Proposed Amendment to Transportation Act of 1920
1925	Before President's Aircraft Board: Aircraft
1925	Relating to Carriage of Goods by Sea
1925	Interest Rates for Carriers
1926	Amendment to Interstate Commerce Act
1926	Railroad Consolidation
1926	Railroad Legislation
1927–1928	Railroad Consolidation
1928	Inland Waterways Corporation: Extension of Barge Line
1928	Transportation Act of 1920: Extension of Government Guaranty to Carriers by Water
1930	Relating to Carriage of Goods by Sea
1930	Motor Carriers, Transportation of Persons in Commerce
1930	Railroad Consolidation, Suspend Authority of ICC to Approve
1931	Railroads: Consolidations and Unifications
1932	Interstate Commerce Act, Amendment
1932	Regulation of Motor Carrier Transportation on Highways

Appendix B-2
Congressional Hearings on
Transportation, 1933–1944

Year	Title
1933	Full Train Crews
1933	Loans to Railroads
1933	Emergency Railroad Transportation Act
1934	Air Commerce Acts, 1926
1934	Prohibition of Free Transportation on Air Lines
1934	Civil Aviation
1934	Amend Section 3 of the Interstate Commerce Act
1934	Regulation of Interstate Motor Buses and Trucks on Public Highways
1935	Regulation of Aircraft Transportation of Passengers and Property
1935	Interstate Regulation of Motor Carriers
1935	Motor Carrier Act of 1935
1935	Extension of Emergency Transportation Act of 1933
1936	Merchant Marine Act of 1936
1939	Transportation Act of 1939
1942	Amend Merchant Marine Act of 1936
1942	Amend National Transportation Act of 1940: Repeal Land Grant Rates on Government Traffic
1943	Railroad Reorganization: Bankruptcy (Section 77)
1943	Federal Regulations of Aeronautics
1944	Abandonment of Railroad Lines

Appendix B-3
Congressional Hearings on
Transportation, 1945–1959

Year	Title
1946	Establish Air Policy Board
1946	Civil Aviation Agreements
1948	Civil Aeronautics Act of 1938
1948	National Transportation Inquiry
1948	Air Regulation
1949	Investigation of Airline Industry
1949	Amendment, Inland Waterways Corporation
1950	Study of Legislation Revising Regulations, Rates and Service in General: Transportation by Land and Water
1951	Civil Aeronautics Board: Legislative Program and Statement of Policies
1952	Transportation Policy
1952	(Same as 1950 Hearings)
1954	Revise Civil Aeronautics Act of 1938
1954	Federal Regulations of Aeronautics
1955	Revise Civil Aeronautics Act of 1938
1955	Transport Policy and Organization
1956	Study of Operations: Civil Aeronautics Administration
1956	Amendment: Merchant Marine Act of 1936
1956	Transportation Policy
1957	Loan Guarantees to Air Carriers
1958	Amend Civil Aeronautics Act
1958	Federal Aviation Act of 1958
1958	Problem Studies: Railroads
1958	Amend Interstate Commerce Act to Provide Rail Routes
1959	Passenger Service Curtailment (Train Discontinuance): Railroads
1959	Transportation Act of 1958: Review of Its Progress as an Amendment to the Interstate Commerce Act
1959	Transportation—Air Carriers
1959	Remove Regulatory Restrictions against Diversification, or Common Ownership of Air, Motor, and Water Carriers

Appendix B-4
Congressional Hearings on
Transportation, 1960–1968

Year	Title
1960	Efficiency and Economy in Government Activities Subcommittee Survey Concerning Aeronautics Board
1960	Amend Section 408(b) Federal Aviation Act to Authorize Elimination of Hearings in Minor Cases
1960	Air Carrier Passenger Privileges or Reduced Rates, Attend to Additional Persons
1960	Amend Federal Aviation Act Relating to Air Carrier Passenger Ticket Rates and Reservations
1961	Government Reorganization: Civil Aeronautics Board
1961	Extension of ICC Loan Guarantee Authority to Railroads
1961	Determination with Respect to Causes of Decline in Regulated Common Carriage as Contrasted to Other Unregulated Types of Carriage
1961	Rule of Rate-making Where Competition between Different Modes of Carriers Is Involved
1961	Determination with Respect to Government Competition with Regulated Surface Carriers
1962	Bill to Repeal Inland Waterways Corporation Act
1962	Bulk Commodity Carriers Moving Certain Agricultural and Fishery Products, and Passengers, by Railway or Highway, Exempt from Minimum Rate Regulation
1963	Bill to Repeal Inland Waterways Corporation Act
1963	Amend Merchant Marine Act with Respect to Restoration to Owners of Government-Requistioned Vessels Constructed under Subsidy Contracts
1963	Transportation Study of St. Lawrence Seaway
1963	Bulk Commodity Carriers Moving Certain Agricultural and Fishing Products and Passengers, Exempt from Minimum Rate Regulation
1963	Problems Associated with Development of Supersonic Transport Program
1963	Federal Aid Proposals Relating to Metropolitan, or Urban, Mass Transportation Problems
1963	National Transportation System
1965	Obsolete War-Built Merchant Marine

Year	*Title*
1965	Assist Common Carriers in Preserving Railroad Passenger Service
1965	Massachusetts, Rhode Island, Connecticut, and New York to Create Their Own Authority for Railroad Passenger Service
1965	Review of Present and Prospective Role of Vertical Type Aircraft: Helicopter Air Service Program
1965	Authorize Secretary of Commerce to Undertake Research and Development Regarding High-Speed Ground Transportation
1965	Motor Carriers and Vehicles
1966	Study with View to Building Stronger Maritime Fleet
1966	Resolution Expressing Intent of Congress with Respect to Right to Review ICC Decision Regarding Passenger Train Discontinuances
1966	Review of ICC Operations Regarding Railroad Safety
1966	Establish Transportation Department with Cabinet Status
1967	Amend Interstate Commerce Act to Clarify Procedures Relating to Passenger Train Discontinuance
1967	Authorize Rehabilitation of Navigation Locks and Appurtenant Structures Located within the United States by the Saint Lawrence Seaway Development Corporation
1967	Study of Maintenance of Adequate Airport System
1967	Establish Through Routes and Joint Rates between Various Modes of Carriage
1968	Plan No. 2: Urban Mass Transportation
1968	Establish National Scenic Rivers System
1968	Study of Effects on Commuter Transportation from Mergers
1968	Authorize Study of Existing and Future Railroad Passenger Service
1968	Air Transportation Safety Study and Recommendations
1968	High-Speed Ground Transportation
1968	Increase Width and Weight Limitations of Vehicles Using Interstate Highway System

Appendix B-5
Congressional Hearings on
Transportation, 1969 to
the Present

Year	Title
1969	Efficiency and Effectiveness of Civil Aeronautics Board
1969	Prohibit Acquisition of Control by Noncarriers of Airlines
1969	Study of Problems and Legislative Proposals to Correct Passenger Trains
1969	Role of Air Carriers in the National Transportation System
1969	Require CAB to Enforce Provision of Certificates Issued to Carriers Providing Adequate Transportation Services
1969	Provide Long-Term Financing for Expanded Programs: Urban Mass Transportation Act
1970	Provide for Long-Range Program of Comprehensive Regional Planning
1970	Emergency Rail Services Act of 1970
1970	Federal Loan Guarantees: Assist Railroads Necessary to National Transportation System
1970	Study of Methods to Reduce Costs of Government Programs, Supersonic Transport Development
1970	Practices and Proposals of CAB with Respect to Group Travel: Air Carrier Fares and Charter Service
1970	Extend High-Speed Ground Transportation Act of 1965 until June 30, 1972
1970	Authorize Establishment of Compacts among States to Create Regional Rail Passenger Service Authorities
1970	Permit Highway Fund Use for Public Transportation Facilities
1970	Establish Transportation Trust Fund to Encourage Urban Mass Transportation
1971	Economic Condition, Air Transportation Industry
1971	Air Transportation Safety Regulations as Administered by FAA
1971	Increase of Bus-Width Limitations on Interstate Highway System
1971	National Facility Compliance Tests for Testing by National Highway Traffic Safety Administration of Motor Vehicles and Equipment
1971	Permit Filing of Motor Carrier Annual Reports to ICC on Basis of 13-Period Accounting Year
1971	AMTRAK (National Railroad Passenger Corporation)
1971	Provide for Purchase of AMTRAK Equipment

Year	Title
1971	Request for Additional Funding of Railroads
1971	Condition of Railroad Industry
1971	Improve, Extend and Insure a Modern Intercity Rail Passenger Network
1971	Extend Railroad Passenger Transportation System to Major Population Areas
1971	Prohibit Discontinuance of Rail Service on Lands Granted by Federal Government
1971	Rail Passenger Service Act of 1970 Amendments: Rail Passenger Network
1971	Grant ICC Power to Authorize One Railroad to Operate Over Tracks of Another in Emergencies
1971	Improve and Insure a Safe and Efficient Surface Transportation System
1971	Extend Transportation Act of 1965 Removing Termination Date
1971	Authorize Establishment of a Class of Limited Air Carriers to Serve Small Communities
1971	Modify National Policy with Respect to Protection of Lands Traversed in Developing Transportation Plans
1971	Extend High-Speed Ground Transportation Act of 1965
1971	Provide for Long-Range Program of Comprehensive Regional Planning and Establish a National Trust Fund
1972	Authorize Free or Reduced Air Rates for Elderly, Handicapped, and Certain Family Members of Airline Employees
1972	Authorize Establishment of a Class of Limited Air Carriers to Serve Small Communities
1972	Provide a Definition for Air and Land Charter Tour Contracts
1972	Authorize Study of Establishing a High-Speed Ground System between the District of Columbia and Annapolis, Maryland
1972	Authorize Study of Establishing a Marine Vessel Transportation System between Baltimore-Annapolis Area in Maryland and Yorktown-Norfolk Area in Virginia
1972	Government Procurements of Transportation from Common Carriers or Forwarders: Auditing and Payment of Charges: Update Procedure and Facilitate
1972	Provide Broader Operating Authority and Flexibility for Certificated Supplemental Air Carriers
1972	Study of Operation, and Recommendations Concerning Increased Assistance to Urban Mass Transportation Systems
1972	Emergency Legislation for Assistance to Assure Adequate Commuter Service in Urban Areas

Year	*Title*
1973	Provide Financial Assistance to AMTRAK
1973	Provide a Definition for Air and Land Charter Tour Contracts
1973	Authorize Feasibility Study of System between Sacramento, San Francisco, Fresno, Los Angeles, and San Diego in State of California
1973	Effect of New Energy Policies on Transportation Industry, Highway Construction, Automobile Industry, etc.
1973	Increase Total Authorized Financial Assistance for Urban Mass Transportation
1973	Emergency Legislation for Assistance to Assure Adequate Commuter Service in Urban Areas
1974	Diversion and Withdrawal of Additional Waters from Lake Michigan into the Illinois Waterway
1974	Federal Subsidy Programs
1974	Report to Congress on Priority Primary Route Cost Study: Highways
1974	Delegate to States Certain Functions with Regard to Navigable Waters, Structures, Excavations, or Fills
1974	Rate-Making Policies and Procedures of the CAB
1974	AMTRAK (National Railroad Passenger Corporation)
1974	Improve AMTRAK Equipment and Services
1974	Regional Rail Reorganization Act
1974	Surface Transportation Legislation
1974	Nominations to the Board of Directors, AMTRAK
1974	Establish a Unified Transportation Assistance Program
1974	Provide Financial Assistance for Fuel Subsidy during Energy Crises and for Other Purposes
1974	Problems of Traveling and Shipping Public Reliant on Common Carriers
1974	Needs and Problems of Mass Transit
1974	Planning and Priorities for the 1970s and Legislation Concerning Assistance Programs, Mass Transit, etc.
1974	Surface Transportation System
1974	Emergency Legislation for Assistance to Assure Adequate Commuter Service in Urban Areas
1974	Establish Unified Transportation Assistance Program
1974	Needs and Problems of Urban Mass Transportation Study
1975	National Highway Needs Report
1975	Amendments of 1975 Airport and Airway Development Act
1975	AMTRAK Improvement Act of 1975
1975	Annual Report on Railroad-High Demonstration Projects

Year	*Title*
1975	Aviation Act of 1975
1975	DOT and Related Agencies Appropriations
1975	Emergency Assistance to Northeast Railroads
1975	Emergency Rail Passenger Service
1975	Emergency Rail Transportation Improvement and Employment Act of 1975
1975	Federal-Aid Highway Act of 1975
1975	Future of the Highway Program
1975	Low-Cost Air Transportation Act
1975	Motor Carrier Reform Act
1975	National Mass Transportation Assistance Act: Amendments
1975	Transportation in Rural America—Meeting Rural Transportation Needs
1975	Railroads—1975 (Five Parts)
1975	Railroad Accounting: Materials Availability and Transportation Statistics
1975	AMTRAK Authorization
1975	Railroad Improvement Act of 1975, Railroad Revitalization Act
1975	Public Works Jobs on the Railroads
1975	Rail Services Act of 1975
1975	Railroad Revitalization Act
1975	Railroad Revitalization and Regulatory Reform Act of 1975
1975	Amendments of Regional Rail Reorganization Act
1975	Regulatory Reform—1974
1975	Second Supplemental Appropriation Bill: DOT
1975	Stimulate Employment Through Railroad Rehabilitation Projects
1975	Final System Plan and Financing for ConRail
1975	Surface Transportation
1975	To Extend and Modify the Airport and Airway Development Act of 1970
1975	U.S. Railway Association Preliminary System Plan
1975	USRA Final System Plan
1976	Acquisition of Rail Properties from ConRail
1976	AMTRAK Improvement Act of 1976
1976	AMTRAK Discontinuance Criteria
1976	Authorizing Extension of the American Canal, Texas
1976	Criteria and Procedures for Making Route and Service Decisions by AMTRAK
1976	DOT Ground Transportation R&D Programs
1976	Making Supplemental Appropriations, FY 76
1976	Rail Amendments of 1976

Year	*Title*
1976	Railroad Revitalization and Regulatory Reform Act of 1976
1976	Rail Transportation Improvement Act
1976	ICC Regulatory Reform
1976	Supplemental Railroad Appropriations
1976	Time Requirements for CAB Applications
1976	To Consider Amendments to Urban Mass Transportation Act of 1964
1976	To Require CAB to Grant Certain Intrastate Air Carriers the Right to Provide Interline Service with Interstate Carriers
1976	Transportation Issues in the Federal Budget for FY 77

Appendix C
Labor Protection Section of Urban Mass Transportation Act

Section 13(c): It shall be a condition of any assistance under section 3 of this Act that fair and equitable arrangements are made, as determined by the Secretary of Labor, to protect the interests of employees affected by such assistance. Such protective arrangements shall include, without being limited to, such provisions as may be necessary for (1) the preservation of rights, privileges, and benefits (including continuation of pension rights and benefits) under existing collective bargaining agreements or otherwise; (2) the continuation of collective bargaining rights; (3) the protection of individual employees against a worsening of their positions with respect to their employment; (4) assurances of employment to employees of acquired mass transportation systems and priority of reemployment of employees terminated or laid off; and (5) paid training or returning programs. Such arrangements shall include provisions protecting individual employees against a worsening of their positions with respect to their employment which shall in no event provide benefits less than those established pursuant to section 5(2)(f) of the Act of February 4, 1887 (24 Stat. 379), as amended. The contract for the granting of any such assistance shall specify the terms and conditions of the protective arrangements.

Source: *Urban Mass Transportation Act of 1964*, as amended through February 5, 1976, U.S. Government Printing Office, Washington, D.C.

About the Author

Harvey A. Levine is a senior associate with R.L. Banks & Associates, Inc., Transportation Consultants, Washington, D.C. He received the B.B.A. degree in transportation from the University of Pittsburgh, the M.B.A. in economics from Duquesne University, and the Ph.D. in business administration from the American University where he was the Fletcher Fellow in Transportation. He has formerly been employed by the New York Central Railroad, Planning Research Corporation, the Department of Transportation, and the Interstate Commerce Commission. He has been a consultant to the U.S. Price Commission, ITT Corporation, several trucking organizations, the National Transportation Policy Study Commission, and a number of other private and public agencies. Dr. Levine is a member of the Transportation Research Forum, and serves on the Committee on Surface Freight Transportation Regulation, Transportation Research Board, and the Financial Management Committee of the American Public Transit Association. His articles have appeared in *Transportation Research Forum Proceedings, Transportation Journal, ICC Practitioners' Journal, Public Utilities Fortnightly*, and *Traffic Quarterly*.